BRIGHTON

TRAVEL GUIDE

2025

Brighton Uncovered—A Stylish Escape to the Seaside Filled with Hidden Gems, Coastal Stories, and Cultural Delights

Abigail I Andrea

Copyright

Table of contents

Copyright

table of contents
Foreword
Welcome to Brighton
Planning Your Trip
Arriving in Brighton
Moving Around the City
Brighton's Distinct Districts
Must-See Landmarks and Experiences
Local Secrets & Hidden Spots
Cultural Highlights and Events
Outdoor Adventures & Nature Escapes
Brighton with Kids
Accommodation in Brighton
Local Flavours and Must-Try Dishes
Where to Eat and Drink
Foodie Activities and Tastings
Where to Shop in Brighton
Suggested Itineraries
Brighton Essentials
Staying Connected
Travel Kindly & Leave No Trace
Day Trips and Nearby Destinations
Photo-Worthy Moments
Packing Smart for Brighton
Emergency & Essential Contacts

Useful Apps and Websites

Farewell Notes

Foreword

Brighton Travel Guide 2025: A Seaside Escape of Culture, Charm & Coastal Adventures

Brighton has always held a certain kind of magic—something you can't quite put your finger on until you've felt the sea breeze on your face while wandering the Palace Pier, or heard the soft strum of a street musician echo through the alleys of North Laine. It's a city where culture and coastline dance together, where history nods politely to modern flair, and where everyone—from solo adventurers to curious families—can find something to love.

This guide was born not just out of research, but out of real footsteps walked across Brighton's pebbled beaches and sun-dappled parks. I remember my first visit—stepping off the train at Brighton Station on a damp spring morning with little more than a backpack and an open weekend ahead. I'd planned to visit the Royal Pavilion, grab a bite of fish and chips, and maybe catch a sunset. What unfolded was something entirely different: I found myself swept up in spontaneous conversations with artists, ducking into tiny record shops, sipping oat milk lattes in converted warehouses, and laughing with strangers in a seafront pub that felt like it had been waiting for me.

Brighton has that effect. It reveals itself not all at once, but in layers—through its people, its passion, its proudly eccentric heartbeat. This guide is for anyone ready to peel back those layers.

Inside, you'll find more than just recommendations—you'll find stories, insights, and a lovingly crafted map of experiences. Whether you're chasing postcard-perfect views, hunting down vegan street food, exploring LGBTQ+ history, or searching for the city's quiet corners, this book was written to help you feel like a local by the sea.

Brighton doesn't ask you to fit in. It simply invites you to be yourself—and somehow, that's where the adventure begins.

Welcome to Brighton.

— **Abigail I Andrea**

Welcome to Brighton

A Coastal Treasure With a Soul

Welcome to Brighton – a city that wraps you in sea-scented air, greets you with open arms, and invites you to be exactly who you are. Perched along England's southern coast, Brighton isn't just a place you visit; it's a place you feel. Known for its colorful personality, inclusive spirit, and charming mix of old-world elegance and contemporary flair, Brighton in 2025 remains one of Britain's most beloved seaside escapes.

Whether you're drawn here by the call of the waves, the pulse of live music echoing from pubs and beach huts, or simply the promise of fish and chips by the sea, Brighton offers a little something for every traveler. This guidebook is your companion to discovering its many layers—and it all begins here.

A Glimpse Into Brighton's Story

Brighton's story begins long before the arrival of hip cafés and art galleries. Once a humble fishing village known as Brighthelmstone, it blossomed into a fashionable seaside resort in the 18th century, when Dr. Richard Russell began prescribing sea bathing as a remedy. Word spread fast, and soon, the city became the darling of the aristocracy—especially after Prince Regent (later King George IV) built the fantastical Royal Pavilion, a palace like no other in England.

Today, traces of that lavish past meet a fiercely independent present. Brighton is now a hub of creativity, diversity, and open-mindedness. You'll see Regency buildings standing beside vegan burger joints, and hear street performers in the Lanes just steps away from the calm hush of historic churches. It's a city with deep roots and fresh blossoms, always evolving yet proudly itself.

First Impressions: Arriving in Brighton

Getting to Brighton is a breeze. Just an hour from London by train, it feels like stepping into a different world. As your train rolls into Brighton Station, you'll catch glimpses of chalky cliffs, the sparkling sea, and rooftops scattered like a mosaic across the South Downs.

Outside the station, the city unfolds in layers. You might spot a local on a bike with a baguette tucked under their arm, a couple strolling hand-in-hand toward the beach, or a busker playing a soulful tune. No matter the time of year, Brighton's air feels alive—with possibility, laughter, and that hard-to-describe but easy-to-feel magic.

Neighborhoods That Welcome You In

Each corner of Brighton hums with its own rhythm. Here's where to begin your discovery:

The Lanes: Brighton's Beating Heart

Wander through this maze of narrow alleyways and you'll feel like you've stepped into a storybook. Independent jewellers, vintage boutiques, and quaint tea houses await around every twist and turn. Don't be surprised if you stumble upon a hidden courtyard café that serves the best scones you've ever tasted.

North Laine: Where Brighton Gets Creative

Bold, brash, and brilliant, North Laine is a magnet for artists, musicians, and free spirits. Think graffiti-covered walls, eco-conscious shops, and buskers playing everything from folk to funk. It's the kind of place where you can sip a turmeric latte, browse records, and pick up a handmade scarf—all in the same afternoon.

Kemptown: The Soul of Brighton's LGBTQ+ Scene

Brighton has long been celebrated for its inclusive and progressive vibe, and Kemptown is at the heart of that. This vibrant district is home to rainbow flags, drag brunches, and some of the friendliest bars in town. It's a neighborhood that celebrates love in all its forms, and you'll feel that in every warm smile and welcoming doorway.

Hove: A Slower Pace, a Seaside Grace

Technically a separate town, Hove is Brighton's elegant twin. Here, things move a little slower. Stroll along the peaceful promenade lined with pastel beach huts, enjoy a picnic in Hove Park, or simply watch the waves roll in. It's the perfect spot for travelers who want charm without the chaos.

Your First Day in Brighton: What Not to Miss

Start your day with a walk along **Brighton Beach**, where the pebbles crunch beneath your shoes and the breeze teases your hair. The iconic **Brighton Palace Pier** stretches out into the sea like a pathway to pure fun—think vintage fairground rides, candy floss, and unbeatable sea views.

Next, wander over to the **Royal Pavilion**, a masterpiece of Indo-Saracenic architecture with onion domes and minarets that seem straight out of a dream. Inside, you'll find dragon chandeliers, Chinese-style wallpaper, and echoes of royal parties long past.

For lunch, why not try a seaside favorite with a twist? Grab **fish and chips** from a local stall and eat it on the beach, or head to a vegan café in North Laine for plant-based delights that don't compromise on flavor.

Wrap up your day with a sunset view from the **British Airways i360**, a soaring glass pod that lifts you above the city for panoramic views that stretch from the coast to the countryside. It's a gentle, stunning reminder of Brighton's blend of tradition and modern innovation.

Local Tips for a Smooth Arrival
* **Currency & Payments**: Brighton uses the British Pound (GBP), and most places accept contactless payments. But it's always wise to

carry a few coins—some charming markets and vintage shops still prefer cash.

* **Transport**: The city is incredibly walkable, but local buses (and even bikes for hire) make it easy to get around. Consider a **Saver Bus Card** if you're staying for several days.

* **Weather**: Brighton weather can change in a heartbeat. Bring layers, a good waterproof jacket, and don't forget sunscreen for those sunny coastal days.

One of Brighton's greatest gifts is its ability to make you feel like you belong. Maybe it's the way locals smile at you in passing, or the shared joy of watching waves crash along the shore. Maybe it's the diversity, or the food, or the music—or maybe it's something you can't quite name.

Whatever draws you here, you'll leave Brighton with more than just memories. You'll carry with you a sense of ease, a bit of salt in your hair, and perhaps even a fresh perspective.

So, take a deep breath of that ocean air. The adventure has just begun.

Planning Your Trip

Set Your Sights on the Seaside
Planning a trip to Brighton is as exciting as the destination itself. This vibrant coastal city, nestled between the rolling South Downs and the English Channel, is effortlessly cool, warmly inclusive, and full of unexpected delights. Whether you're traveling solo, bringing the whole family, planning a romantic escape, or looking for a fun-filled weekend with friends, Brighton in 2025 welcomes you with a fresh sea breeze and a hundred ways to make your visit unforgettable.

But before you stroll along the pier with an ice cream in hand or tuck into a beachside brunch, a little thoughtful preparation will go a long way. This chapter will guide you through the essentials—when to go, how to get there, what to pack, where to stay, and how to make the most of your time in this charming, culture-soaked city.

Best Times to Visit Brighton
Brighton's charm is year-round, but the experience changes with the seasons. Here's what to expect:

Spring (March to May):
This is when Brighton begins to bloom. The weather is mild, daffodils brighten the parks, and there's a buzz of anticipation in the air. It's a great time for walking the Undercliff Path or exploring the Royal Pavilion Gardens without summer crowds.

Summer (June to August):
Peak season brings sunshine, beach festivals, and late evenings filled with live music and laughter. You'll find Brighton's streets buzzing with tourists and locals alike. Pack your swimsuit, sunscreen, and patience for queues at popular spots—it's all worth it.

Autumn (September to November):
The city slows down just enough for you to breathe it all in. The sea air turns crisp, and cozy cafés become irresistible. September often has lovely weather and fewer crowds, making it a sweet spot for travelers.

Winter (December to February):
Brighton doesn't hibernate. Winter brings moody seascapes, twinkling lights in The Lanes, and fewer tourists. It's ideal for a peaceful retreat. Wrap up warm and enjoy hot

chocolate with sea views or explore the indie theatre scene.

Getting to Brighton

Brighton is surprisingly accessible, making it a stress-free destination for both domestic and international travelers.

From London:

Brighton is just about an hour from London by train. Trains depart frequently from London Victoria, London Bridge, and Blackfriars. It's one of the easiest day trips from the capital, but we recommend staying a few days to truly soak it in.

From Abroad:

If you're flying into the UK, **Gatwick Airport** is the closest international hub—only 30 minutes away by direct train. Heathrow and London City airports are also manageable, though the journey takes a bit longer.

By Car:

Driving into Brighton offers flexibility but comes with one caveat: parking. The city center has limited and often pricey parking options. If you're driving, book accommodation with parking or look into park-and-ride services.

By Coach:
National Express and other long-distance bus companies offer budget-friendly travel from London and major UK cities. The coach station is centrally located on Pool Valley, near the seafront.

Where to Stay: Finding Your Brighton Base

Brighton offers a wide variety of accommodation, from charming guest houses to luxury hotels and quirky Airbnb rentals. Consider what vibe you're after:

Seafront Stays:
If waking up to the sound of waves is your dream, book a room along Kings Road or Marine Parade. Options range from classic Victorian hotels to modern beach apartments.

The Lanes & North Laine:
Perfect for those who love to be in the middle of it all. Stay here for boutique hotels, cozy B\&Bs, and proximity to shops, restaurants, and nightlife.

Kemptown:
Brighton's LGBTQ+ heart is also one of the best places for community-centered stays.

Expect vibrant guesthouses, welcoming hosts, and a real sense of belonging.

Hove:
A quieter, more residential experience. Ideal for families or those seeking peace without being too far from the action.

Tip: Book early if you're visiting during summer or for big events like Brighton Pride or The Fringe Festival. Accommodations fill up fast!

What to Pack: The Brighton Basics

Brighton weather is famously changeable. Locals joke that you can experience all four seasons in a single day—and they're not wrong. Pack smart:

* **Layers:** A light jacket, scarf, and sweater will serve you well year-round.
* **Comfortable shoes:** Whether it's the pebbly beach or cobbled streets, Brighton rewards good footwear.
* **Reusable water bottle & tote bag:** The city is big on sustainability.
* **Swimwear & sunglasses (in summer):** For that refreshing dip in the sea.

* **Umbrella or raincoat:** Just in case. This **is** the UK, after all.

Navigating Brighton: Getting Around

Brighton is compact, walkable, and pedestrian-friendly. Still, there are a few options to make your movements smoother:

On Foot:
Most of Brighton's highlights are within walking distance of each other. Exploring by foot lets you discover hidden gems and unexpected moments.

By Bike:
Brighton's cycle lanes and rental services (like BTN BikeShare) make it easy to cruise around town. You can even cycle along the seafront for stunning views.

Buses:
The local bus system, run by Brighton & Hove Buses, is reliable and covers everything from central Brighton to the surrounding hills. Download the app for real-time info and digital ticketing.

Travel Tech and Handy Tools

Technology can make your trip smoother and more fun. Here are some apps and websites worth downloading before you arrive:

* **Brighton & Hove Buses App:** Real-time schedules, journey planning, and tickets.
* **Citymapper:** Offers easy-to-follow local transport routes.
* **Google Maps & Offline Maps:** Perfect for navigating winding lanes.
* **Tripadvisor & TimeOut Brighton:** Great for reviews and current event listings.
* **Brighton Festival App (in season):** For booking shows, workshops, and exhibitions.

Smart Tips From Locals

* **Buy Local:** Visit independent shops and support Brighton's creative community.
* **Avoid Seafront Cafés at Lunchtime on Weekends:** They fill up fast. Try heading a few streets inland for equally delicious and often quieter spots.
* **Catch the Sunset from Brighton Beach:** Especially in late spring or early autumn—it's magical.

Planning your trip to Brighton isn't about ticking boxes—it's about preparing for a city that dances to its own rhythm. From the moment you arrive, you'll sense that Brighton is more than a destination. It's an experience crafted from sea spray, music, creativity, and a deep-seated love for individuality.

Take your time. Embrace the unexpected. And let Brighton unfold for you, one delightful detail at a time.

Arriving in Brighton

Welcome, You've Made It!

Whether you've journeyed an hour from London or crossed an ocean to get here, there's something incredibly rewarding about stepping into Brighton for the first time. That first breath of sea air—crisp, salty, and tinged with the smell of fresh fish and distant coffee—marks the beginning of your coastal adventure.

Arriving in a new city can bring a mix of excitement and uncertainty. But here in Brighton, things unfold with ease. The city is used to welcoming newcomers—from sun-seeking tourists to curious day-trippers and international visitors in search of its renowned creative energy. In this chapter, we'll help you navigate your arrival—whether by train, car, coach, or air—and give you a smooth start to your Brighton journey with practical tips, friendly suggestions, and a few local secrets along the way.

Your Gateway to the Coast: How to Get to Brighton

By Train – The Fast Track from London and Beyond. Brighton Station, perched slightly above the city on Queens Road, is the most common arrival point for visitors. It's a handsome Victorian structure that feels both grand and grounded—an excellent introduction to the city's fusion of history and modernity.

From **London**, trains leave every 10 to 15 minutes from **Victoria Station**, **London Bridge**, and **Blackfriars**, reaching Brighton in just under an hour. If you're coming from **Gatwick Airport**, a direct train will have you at the coast in about 30 minutes—no transfers needed.

Once you arrive, you're perfectly placed: the station is just a 10-minute downhill walk to the seafront, passing cafes, boutiques, and glimpses of the sea as you go.

> **Local tip:** If you arrive hungry, pop into Café Coho across from the station or head straight down to North Laine for your pick of brunch spots and bakeries.

By Car – Road-Tripping to the Seaside. Driving into Brighton is scenic and direct, especially if you're coming down the **A23** from London or the **A27** from the east or west. The city is well-signposted, and as you approach, you'll see the blue-gray sea stretching across the horizon.

That said, **parking** can be a bit of a puzzle. Much of the city is residential with limited paid parking zones. If your accommodation offers parking—great, use it. If not, consider these options:

* **Churchill Square Car Park:** Central, close to shops and the beach.
* **Brighton Marina Car Park:** Free parking up to 24 hours, with regular buses into the city center.
* **Park & Ride:** Brighton currently has limited park-and-ride facilities, but you can park on the outskirts (like Withdean Stadium) and take a bus in.

> **Driving tip:** The roads in The Lanes and North Laine are narrow and often one-way. If you're navigating the city by car, use a GPS and keep calm—Brighton's charm includes a few quirky turns.

By Coach – Budget-Friendly and Comfortable. For travelers watching their budget or coming from afar, coach services like **National Express** or **Megabus** offer direct routes into Brighton. The coach station at **Pool Valley**, near the Old Steine, places you just minutes from the iconic Brighton Pier and the beach.

It's a no-fuss way to arrive, especially if you're carrying luggage—everything you need is within walking distance from here, including taxis, buses, and cafés to regroup after your journey.

By Air – Flying in and Connecting Smoothly. Brighton doesn't have its own airport, but it's well-connected through nearby **Gatwick Airport**, which is only about 30 minutes away by train. Gatwick is an international hub with flights from Europe, North America, the Middle East, and beyond.

If you land at **Heathrow**, it's about 90 minutes by public transport (train or coach). You can take the Heathrow Express to Paddington, transfer to the Tube or another train line, and then head south to Brighton.

For travelers landing at **London City** or **Stansted**, the journey is longer, but still manageable with train or coach connections.

First Impressions: Finding Your Feet in the City. Once your feet hit the Brighton pavement, take a moment to settle in. Here are a few simple steps to make your arrival smooth and stress-free:

Find Your Bearings

Brighton's layout is refreshingly walkable. The main areas—**Brighton Station**, **North Laine**, **The Lanes**, **Kemptown,** and **Hove**—are all connected by footpaths, local buses, or short taxi rides.

You can orient yourself by heading toward the sea. Most streets slope downward from the train station to the seafront, with Queens Road and West Street acting as main arteries into town.

Pick Up a Local SIM or Connect to Wi-Fi

Most cafes and hotels offer free Wi-Fi. If you're staying longer or need reliable data, stop by a mobile shop along Western Road or in Churchill Square to grab a prepaid SIM card.

Grab an E-Bike or Scooter

Brighton in 2025 is embracing green transport. You'll see **electric scooters** and **BTN BikeShare cycles** parked throughout the city. They're perfect for zipping along the beach or getting from the Marina to the Palace Pier.

> **Safety reminder:** Scooters are for riders 18+, and helmets are strongly encouraged. Cycle lanes are well-marked along the seafront and major roads.

Currency, Language, and Local Etiquette

Money Matters

Brighton uses the British pound (GBP). Credit and debit cards are widely accepted, including contactless payments. You'll rarely need cash, but if you do, ATMs are scattered around town—especially on Western Road and North Street.

Language and Manners

English is the spoken language, but Brighton's international vibe means you'll hear French, Spanish, Polish, and more. Locals are friendly, informal, and often happy to chat.

Brightonians tend to be relaxed but respectful. Queueing is sacred, tipping (10–15% in restaurants) is appreciated, and a cheerful "Cheers!" goes a long way.

First-Day Essentials

Here are a few practical tasks to consider after arriving:

* **Check into your accommodation early if possible**—many hotels offer bag drop if your room's not ready.
* **Swing by the VisitBrighton Information Point** on the seafront near the Palace Pier. They offer maps, attraction tickets, and friendly advice.
* **Stock up on local snacks and supplies** from **Infinity Foods** (for organic bites) or **Hisbe Supermarket** (an ethical alternative to big chains).
* **Book your activities ahead** if you're visiting during peak season. Walking tours, escape rooms, and afternoon teas fill up quickly.

Arriving in Brighton is the start of a slower, more soulful pace. Unlike big cities that demand urgency, Brighton invites you to breathe. Walk the beach. Duck into a record store. Sip a flat white under fairy lights. There's no wrong way to begin—just step into the rhythm of the waves and let the city reveal itself, moment by moment.

This is your arrival—not just into a place, but into a feeling. One of welcome, warmth, and wide-open possibility.

Moving Around the City

Strolling by the Sea and Beyond

In Brighton, movement isn't just about getting from A to B—it's a part of the experience. You'll pass pastel-painted houses, hidden gardens, street performers under rainbow bunting, and salty sea air that seems to carry music from a distance. Whether you're hopping on a bike, catching a bus, or simply wandering on foot, Brighton makes getting around feel relaxed, intuitive, and often quite scenic.

The city is compact enough to explore at a leisurely pace but dynamic enough to offer a few transportation options depending on where you're headed. In this chapter, we'll walk (and ride) you through the best ways to navigate Brighton and Hove like a local—without the stress.

Walking: The Brighton Way of Life

Let's start with what many visitors find becomes their favorite mode of travel—walking. Brighton is made for pedestrians. You can easily walk from the train station to the beach in under 15 minutes. The stroll takes you past quirky boutiques in North Laine, the majestic

Theatre Royal, and the Royal Pavilion's onion domes—all before you catch your first glimpse of the Channel.

The Lanes are best explored on foot. This maze of medieval alleyways invites you to slow down and meander between vintage jewelers, fudge shops, and cafes barely wider than their doorways. Don't be surprised if you spend an hour there just window shopping and people-watching.

> **Tip for walkers:** Wear comfy shoes. The streets are mostly flat, but there are some cobblestones and inclines—especially if you head toward the station or up to the residential hills of Hanover or Queen's Park.

BTN BikeShare and E-Scooters: Zip Along the Promenade.
For those wanting to cover a little more ground without jumping in a car, **Brighton's BikeShare scheme**—affectionately known as **BTN Bikes**—is a fantastic option. Stations are located across the city, especially along the beach, in central neighborhoods, and near student areas.

The new **electric-assist models** (launched in late 2024) make climbing the hills between Kemp Town and Seven Dials a breeze. Just download the app, locate a bike, and you're good to go. Rates are affordable, and bikes can be dropped off at any docking station.

Meanwhile, Brighton's **e-scooter scheme**, tried successfully over the past few years, is now a permanent fixture. You'll see scooters lined up near Brighton Pier, at the Marina, and by Brighton Dome. These are ideal for quick trips—say, from the i360 to your hotel or from Hove Lawns to the Royal Pavilion.

> **Local insight:** Cycling along the **Undercliff Walk** from the Marina to Saltdean is a stunning ride—cliffs on one side, waves crashing below on the other. Just check the tide times first!

Buses: Reliable, Colorful, and Coastal
Brighton & Hove Buses are more than just public transport—they're part of the city's identity. With names like "The Regency Route" and buses painted in cheerful reds and creams, they're charming, regular, and surprisingly efficient.

The **city's bus network** connects nearly every neighborhood—from the hills of Hollingbury to the posh lanes of Hove. Routes run frequently along major corridors like Western Road and Lewes Road, and you can use contactless payment directly on board.

Two standout routes for travelers:

* **Route 77:** The scenic bus to **Devil's Dyke**, perfect for a countryside escape with sweeping views of the South Downs.
* **Route 12/12X:** This coastal ride takes you east to **Rottingdean** or west to **Shoreham**, with views of cliffs and sea all the way.

> **Practical tip:** The Brighton & Hove Buses app offers real-time tracking, fare info, and even live crowd levels so you can pick a quiet seat on top.

Taxis and Ride Shares: When Convenience Counts. While most of Brighton is walkable, sometimes you'll want a quick ride home after a night out or need to carry luggage to your accommodation. Taxis are easy to spot—especially near Brighton Station and the seafront—and are regulated for safety and price consistency.

Ride-share services like **Uber** and **Bolt** also operate in Brighton and are often slightly cheaper than taxis, particularly during off-peak times. They're a useful backup late at night or when public transport has stopped.

> **Brightonian courtesy:** Always say "Cheers, mate" to your driver. It's a small thing, but it goes a long way in this friendly city.

Trains: For Day Trips and Distant Corners
You probably arrived by train, and it's worth remembering that **Brighton Station** isn't just a gateway in—it's also your link to a wealth of easy day trips.

* **To Lewes:** A 15-minute train ride takes you to this historic town of castle ruins and antique shops.
* **To London:** Perfect for a day of museums and theatre before retreating back to the quieter coast.
* **To Worthing or Eastbourne:** Both offer quieter seaside experiences with their own charm.

Brighton Station also connects you to outer neighborhoods like Preston Park and Falmer, home of the University of Sussex and the Amex Stadium (for football fans).

> **Train tip:** Trains can get busy during summer weekends and rush hour. If you want a seat with a sea view, aim for off-peak hours.

Neighborhood Know-How: Getting Around Local Spots. Here's how to navigate some of Brighton's most popular neighborhoods:

* **North Laine:** Best explored on foot or bike. This area is tight-knit with lots of independent shops and coffee spots. Great for aimless wandering.
* **The Lanes:** A walking maze. Use local landmarks like the clock tower or Pavilion to reorient yourself—GPS doesn't always cooperate here!
* **Kemptown:** East of the pier and a little uphill. Walkable, but a bus or scooter saves time if you're headed to the Marina or Saltdean.
* **Hove:** Wider streets and leafy avenues make this ideal for biking. Head west from Brighton Pier and watch the promenade slowly transform into Hove Lawns' relaxed vibe.

Accessibility and Inclusive Transport

Brighton makes a consistent effort to be inclusive. Most buses and stations are wheelchair accessible, and BTN Bikes has added adaptive bike models for different mobility needs. Many crossings have tactile paving and audio cues, and attractions like the i360, Pavilion, and Brighton Museum are all accessible-friendly.

> **Resource:** The **Brighton Access Guide** (available online and at the Tourist Information Point) includes up-to-date info on accessible routes and services.

Whether you're racing toward Devil's Dyke on a double-decker bus or dawdling through the Lanes with an ice cream in hand, Brighton lets you move at the speed of your own curiosity. The city doesn't rush you. It encourages detours. It whispers, "Go on, have a look down that alley. Take the long way home."

So rent a bike, hop on a bus, walk barefoot in the pebbles, or just sit at a café and watch everyone else go by. However you choose to move around Brighton, you're doing it right.

Brighton's Distinct Districts

A Patchwork of Personality by the Sea

Brighton isn't just one place—it's a lively mosaic stitched together by stories, history, and the untamed energy of the sea. Wander a few streets in any direction and you'll feel like you've entered an entirely new world. Bohemian lanes humming with guitar strings give way to quiet crescents echoing the footsteps of Victorian poets. Hilltop hideaways overlook pebble-strewn beaches, and rainbow-painted terraces look out across tidy Georgian squares.

To truly understand Brighton is to explore it district by district. Each area has its own heartbeat, its own rhythm, its own way of catching the light. Let's take a stroll through Brighton's neighborhoods, each a chapter in this coastal city's story.

The Lanes: A Twisting Time Capsule

If Brighton has a soul, it might be tucked somewhere within **The Lanes**. This centuries-old tangle of narrow passageways sits just inland from the seafront, and its atmosphere is nothing short of enchanting. Think cobblestones slick with rain, hanging baskets overflowing with flowers, and a saxophone's tune drifting out of a hidden courtyard.

Once a humble fishing village called Brighthelmstone, this area still holds the bones of its medieval past. But in 2025, it's also a playground of goldsmiths, tailors, vintage perfumeries, and cozy bistros tucked behind ivy-covered doors.

> **Don't Miss: Choccywoccydoodah** may be long gone, but **Savannah Artisan Chocolates** has filled its shoes with sculpted cocoa creations. For a perfect people-watching perch, grab a table at **Blackbird Tea Rooms**, where lace doilies and floral teacups transport you straight to a gentler time.

North Laine: Brighton's Bohemian Canvas
Just north of The Lanes lies **North Laine**—Brighton beating creative hearts. This neighborhood is a symphony of street art, second-hand record shops, vegan bakeries, and rainbow flags fluttering proudly from balconies. The buildings are lower here,

cheekier in posture, and brimming with colour and character.

It's the kind of place where a vintage Levi's rack sits beside a psychic's storefront, where graffiti isn't vandalism but a local artist's calling card. On weekends, the lanes swell with slow-moving crowds, all sipping cold brews or juggling armfuls of thrift-store finds.

> **Local Story:** You might spot **"Zebra Man",** a beloved Brightonian who paints his beard black and white and roams North Laine in full safari suit. Locals say he's lived here for decades, becoming something of a human landmark.

> **Top Tip:** Visit on a weekday morning for a calmer vibe. Drop into **Resident Music** for records and artist recs, then grab a turmeric latte at **Pelicano**, while watching the street unfold before you.

Kemptown: Eccentric, Elegant, and Effortlessly Cool. To the east of the city centre lies Kemptown, where elegance meets edge. This neighborhood sweeps upward from the seafront in a gentle hill crowned with white Regency crescents. It's Brighton's unofficial

LGBTQ+ district, but its draw is universal: inclusive, arty, and full of flair.

Here, drag brunches share the calendar with candlelit classical concerts, and antique stores brush shoulders with avant-garde galleries. Kemptown is where Brighton lets its freak flag fly, with a wink and a knowing nod.

> **Where to Go:** Spend a lazy morning in **St. George's Road**, rummaging through **The Open Market's** antiques or tucking into a warm croissant at **Busby & Wilds**. Then make your way down to the under-the-radar **Duke's Mound Beach**, a quieter patch of pebbles popular with locals and a hotspot for sunset photographers.

Seven Dials and Montpelier: Elegant Hills and Garden Squares. Head northwest from the centre and the buzz gradually gives way to leafy tranquility. **Seven Dials**, perched atop a gentle rise, is Brighton's little urban village—charming, walkable, and just far enough from the bustle to exhale deeply. With its circular junction at the heart (the "dials"), the area fans out into leafy streets lined with Edwardian terraces and secret gardens.

Just beyond lies **Montpelier**, a Georgian gem of high-ceilinged homes and broad boulevards. It's a neighborhood that whispers rather than shouts, where children's laughter echoes in hidden parks and locals swap gardening tips over fences.

> **Traveler Tip:** For a taste of Brighton's refined side, walk down **Vernon Terrace** toward **Montpelier Crescent**—the architecture is postcard-perfect. Stop for brunch at **The Flour Pot Bakery** on Dyke Road, where fresh pastries and friendly chats are the norm.

Hove: The Quiet Counterpart. "Hove, actually." You'll hear this phrase with a smile when someone from Hove corrects a visitor who assumes they live in Brighton proper. And it sums up the place perfectly—wry, charming, and just a little bit proud.

While Brighton buzzes, **Hove** paces itself. Think broad avenues, beach huts in mint condition, and a promenade less populated but just as scenic. Families picnic on Hove Lawns. Joggers follow the sea wall past Art Deco buildings. And dogs outnumber seagulls.

This is Brighton's gentler half—a place to breathe, read, and linger.

> **Experience This:** Visit Hove Museum & Art Gallery, tucked in a Victorian villa. It's free, under-visited, and packed with charming oddities—from vintage toys to contemporary crafts. Afterwards, enjoy an ice cream at **Marrocco's,** a local institution since 1969.

Hanover and Queen's Park: Brighton's Hilltop Hideaways.If you're feeling adventurous—and up for a bit of a climb—make your way to **Hanover**, a hilltop district known for its cheerful rows of pastel-painted terraces and community spirit. It feels like a small town within a city, where cats sunbathe on windowsills and neighbors gather for monthly "Hanover Day" street parties.

Just downhill, **Queen's Park** is built around a large green space complete with a duck pond, dog walkers, and a café that does an excellent bacon bap. The area has a quiet charm and is a great base if you're after something residential and real.

> **Insider Tip:** The **Hanover Community Pub Trail** is a beloved local tradition. There

are at least a dozen pubs scattered across the steep lanes—each with character, and many dog-friendly. Start at **The Greys** or **The Haus on the Hill**, and see where the night takes you.

Brighton Marina: Modern Waterside Living. To the far east, Brighton Marina is a different beast entirely—modern, slick, and filled with the gentle clatter of moored boats. Built in the 1970s and constantly evolving, this area is Brighton's waterside playground. It's where you'll find chain restaurants, a cinema, bowling alley, and some surprisingly luxurious yacht-side apartments.

It's not as soul-stirring as The Lanes or as photogenic as Kemptown, but it has its place—especially for families, film-goers, or anyone keen to rent a paddleboard and glide out to sea.

> **Evening Recommendation:** Book a table at **Malmaison's Chez Mal**, where dinner comes with marina views and sea air. Then wander the boardwalk with a gelato, watching the boats gently bob in the moonlight.

Each district in Brighton tells a different story. Some sing in colour, some whisper through architecture, and others simply invite you to stay awhile, soak it in, and return again. Whether you're searching for vintage treasures in North Laine, sipping a cocktail in Kemptown, or watching the sun melt into the sea at Hove, one thing's for sure:

You'll find a version of Brighton that feels like it was waiting just for you.

Must-See Landmarks and Experiences

Unforgettable Moments by the Sea
Brighton isn't just a destination—it's a vibrant, beating heart of culture, color, and coastal wonder. The city's landmarks are more than just places to see—they're invitations to feel, to explore, to wonder. From ornate royal palaces to otherworldly art installations, Brighton blends history with creativity, elegance with eccentricity. If you're only in town for a few days, these are the moments and monuments that will etch themselves into your memory long after the tide has rolled out.

The Royal Pavilion:
Imagine walking into a dream spun from the threads of Indian, Chinese, and Regency fantasy. That's the sensation of stepping into the Royal Pavilion, one of Brighton's most iconic and extravagant landmarks. Built in the early 1800s as a seaside retreat for the flamboyant Prince Regent (later George IV), the Pavilion is an architectural marvel unlike anything else in Britain.

On the outside, onion domes and minarets gleam in the sun, rising above manicured gardens like a mirage. Step inside, and you're transported to a world of opulence: dragon chandeliers, silk-lined walls, and banquet halls so lavish they feel more fairy tale than real life.

> **Travel Tip:** Take the audio tour—it's filled with quirky historical details and juicy royal gossip. And don't skip the Pavilion Gardens afterward; they're a peaceful spot for a takeaway lunch from nearby **Pavilion Gardens Café.**

Brighton Palace Pier: Classic Fun with a Salty Breeze. No trip to Brighton is complete without a wander down the **Brighton Palace Pier**. Opened in 1899, it's part carnival, part seascape, and pure seaside magic. The moment you step onto the wooden planks and hear the distant ding of arcade machines and the squawk of gulls overhead, you know you've arrived.

There's something for everyone here—traditional fish and chips, candy floss, roller coaster rides, and slot machines that haven't changed in decades. The views at the far end are worth the stroll alone: the city to one side, the endless blue horizon to the other.

> **Local Tip:** Visit just before sunset. The lights begin to twinkle, the sea reflects the golden sky, and the whole pier comes alive in a dreamy, nostalgic glow.

Brighton i360: Towering 162 meters above the beach, the **Brighton i360** is a futuristic marvel that offers the best panoramic views of the city, the South Downs, and the English Channel. Designed by the creators of the London Eye, this glass viewing pod gently ascends into the sky like a modern-day airship.

In 2025, the i360 has doubled down on its "flight" theme. The new Sky Bar serves sparkling wine and local gin as you rise, making the experience feel more like a glamorous launch party than a simple observation tower.

> **Don't Miss:** On clear days, you can spot the Isle of Wight to the west and cliffs of Beachy Head to the east. Book the **Sunset Flight** for maximum wow factor.

Brighton's Street Art Scene: While Brighton's galleries are worth visiting, its most electric artworks live outdoors. The city is a living canvas, splashed with murals, political statements, portraits, and psychedelic explosions of color. Some pieces are commissions; others are acts of raw expression. All are part of the city's living, breathing art scene.

You'll find standout works in **North Laine**, where nearly every alley and brick wall has a story. Keep an eye out for the ever-evolving **Banksy-inspired pieces** near Kensington Street, and the massive sea creature murals on Trafalgar Lane.

> **Experience It:** Book a street art walking tour led by local artists. You'll hear the meanings behind the murals and even get to spray your own (legally!) on designated walls.

Undercliff Walk: A Journey Between Cliffs and Sea. For a dose of natural drama, the **Undercliff Walk** is one of Brighton's most exhilarating coastal experiences. This pedestrian-only path hugs the base of towering white chalk cliffs, stretching from **Brighton Marina** to the charming village of **Saltdean**.

The sound of crashing waves on one side and chalk cliffs looming on the other creates a sense of cinematic awe. Along the way, you'll pass seaweed-covered rock pools, tidal shelves, and occasionally, brave swimmers leaping into the bracing water.

> **Travel Tip:** Start early to catch the light slanting across the cliffs, and end with a seaside brunch at **The Saltdean Tavern** or an ocean dip at the Saltdean Lido, recently restored and glorious in the sun.

Volk's Electric Railway: Hop aboard the **world's oldest operating electric railway**, first launched in 1883 by inventor Magnus Volk. The charming narrow-gauge **Volk's Electric Railway** zips along the seafront between the Palace Pier and Brighton Marina.

Though modest in speed, this ride is full of charm and nostalgia. The restored cars rattle and hum, offering a delightful throwback experience with views across the pebbled beach and glittering water.

> **Family-Friendly Bonus:** Kids adore the open-air ride, and it's a relaxing way to get between two major attractions.

Brighton Dome and Corn Exchange: The Beating Heart of Culture. Adjacent to the Royal

Pavilion is the **Brighton Dome**, a spectacular performance venue with a past as colorful as the shows it hosts. Once a royal stables complex, it's now home to everything from ballet and comedy to world music and TED-style talks.

In 2025, the recent restoration of the **Corn Exchange** has transformed it into a state-of-the-art cultural space while preserving its historic grandeur. High ceilings, elegant detailing, and modern acoustics create an immersive setting for performances you'll talk about for years.

> **Planning Tip:** Book tickets in advance—shows often sell out, especially during the **Brighton Festival** in May, when the whole city becomes a stage.

Brighton's landmarks aren't just places—they're moments waiting to happen. Whether you're gazing down from the clouds in the i360, getting lost in the echoes of royal footsteps at the Pavilion, or laughing over a cone of chips on the pier, these experiences are the essence of Brighton.

They tell the story of a city that's both grand and quirky, historic and ever-changing. A place where every corner hums with possibility and where the sea is always just a few steps away.

So bring your curiosity, your camera, and your sense of wonder—Brighton's magic is ready for you.

Local Secrets & Hidden Spots

Here's a little secret: Brighton saves some of its best treasures for those willing to dig a little deeper. Beyond the palace domes, pebble beaches, and rainbow-bright streets lie quiet courtyards, cozy corners, and surprises tucked between the cracks of the city's familiar face.

If you've ever walked down a narrow lane and wondered, "Where does that go?"—this chapter is for you. Let's dive into the charming, quirky, and quietly magical places that Brighton locals love but rarely shout about.

The Lanes' Secret Passages and Hidden Courtyards

The Lanes are famous, yes—but **within** the Lanes, there are secrets even locals occasionally overlook. Slip past the jewelry shops and cafes, and you'll find a maze of tucked-away twittens (that's Sussex-speak for narrow alleyways) and unexpectedly quiet courtyards.

One gem is **Meeting House Lane's** lesser-known passage that leads to a peaceful courtyard with ivy-wrapped walls and the barely-there scent of lavender from hanging pots. There's often a street musician playing something gentle—violin, flute, maybe even saw music if you're lucky. This is the spot to pause with a cinnamon bun from **Sugardough Bakery** and simply watch the shadows change on the cobbles.

> **Insider Tip:** Keep an eye out for Post House Passage—blink and you'll miss it. It leads to a petite courtyard of old flint cottages that feels like a slice of 18th-century Brighton.

St. Ann's Well Gardens: A Lush, Local Sanctuary. While tourists picnic in the Pavilion Gardens, Brighton residents head uphill to **St. Ann's Well Gardens** in Hove. It's a lush, leafy escape filled with winding paths, trickling springs, a secret apiary, and squirrels that are far too confident for their own good.

In spring and summer, the gardens explode with color—camellias, bluebells, and wild garlic among the towering trees. A small but charming café near the tennis courts serves oat milk flat whites and fresh pastries, often accompanied by the chatter of dogs and their humans after morning walks.

> **Fun Fact:** The gardens were once a Victorian health spa destination, believed to have healing spring water. There's still a well on site, though it's mostly a wishing well now—don't drink from it!

The Ghost Village Beneath the Sea: On the cliffs east of Brighton Marina lies **Roedean**, home to a posh girls' school, an underappreciated coastal walk, and—if local legend is to be believed—a network of tunnels once used during World War II. Some whisper of a sunken village or smuggler hideouts beneath the cliffs, though much remains unconfirmed and thrillingly mysterious.

What is certain is that a few disused ventilation shafts and sealed tunnel entrances peek out from the chalk cliffs. While you can't go exploring inside (they're fenced for safety), the walk along **Roedean Undercliff Path** is full of intrigue, with dramatic sea views and the faint scent of salt and stories.

> **Traveler's Thrill:** Head there at low tide for a glimpse of sea-sculpted caves below the

cliffs. Bring sturdy shoes—and a wild imagination.

Kensington Gardens on a Rainy Afternoon

Brighton has a curious way of becoming more interesting in the rain, especially around **Kensington Gardens** in the North Laine. The covered arcades and quirky shop fronts take on a cozy glow, and the smell of second-hand books, incense, and just-roasted coffee rises into the drizzle.

Wander into **Raining Books**, a blink-and-you-miss-it upstairs bookstore, where the creaky floors and handwritten labels make browsing feel like a treasure hunt. Or duck into **Snoopers Paradise**, Brighton's legendary antiques bazaar. One moment you're examining a Victorian postcard collection, the next you've found a tray of 1970s sunglasses or a rotary telephone in perfect condition.

> **Local Ritual:** Grab a cup of tea from **Bluebird Tea Co.**, then head upstairs in Snoopers to the vintage photobooth. You'll emerge with a strip of grainy portraits and, more likely than not, a new favorite memory.

Brighton's Secret Beach

Believe it or not, Brighton has a quieter beach—it just doesn't look like one from above. Head east of the Marina and follow the undercliff path until you reach a spot where the chalk cliffs stretch dramatically above and the crowds thin out. This is **Ovingdean Gap**, a semi-secret shingle beach where locals come to swim, sketch, or simply sit in stillness.

Seals have been spotted here in the early mornings, and during the late afternoon, the golden light hits the cliffs with an almost cinematic warmth. There's a tiny café—**The Ovingdean Beach Café**—that makes what many say is the best bacon bap on the coast. We're not here to argue.

> **Quiet Tip:** Go on a weekday morning for the full secret-beach feel. The pebbles crunch underfoot, the wind hums through the cliffs, and for a moment, it's just you and the sea.

The Candlelit Charm of The Plotting Parlour

Brighton has its share of buzzing pubs and glitzy bars, but when you want something intimate, seek out The Plotting Parlour. Tucked down a narrow street near Old Steine, this cocktail lounge has the vibe of a speakeasy, with velvet chairs, moody lighting, and menus hidden inside old books.

It's the kind of place where the bartender asks what you feel like drinking and then creates something spectacular just for you—think lavender and lemon gin fizzes or smoky mezcal cocktails topped with a flamed orange peel.

> **Evening Escape:** Arrive early and get a corner booth. It's where many Brighton love stories have quietly begun.

Brighton rewards curiosity. It's a city layered with stories—some out in the open, others waiting behind secret doors or halfway down forgotten lanes. To find them, slow down. Wander without a map. Follow your instincts (or that oddly-dressed person with a paintbrush sticking out of their tote bag—they probably know a great spot).

This chapter isn't just a guide—it's an invitation. Get lost. Be nosy. Ask the person behind the counter what they love most about this place. Chances are, they'll tell you something amazing—and then you'll have a secret to pass along, too.

Cultural Highlights and Events

Brighton's Beating Heart

In Brighton, culture isn't something that happens behind velvet ropes or gallery glass—it pulses through the streets, blares from basement gigs, beams from theatre spotlights, and dances in parades that spill through the city like waves of joy. It's a place where creativity doesn't just live—it thrives in full technicolour, every day of the year.

Whether you arrive during a festival frenzy or a quiet off-season evening, there's always something happening. Brighton doesn't need a reason to celebrate—it just does. And in 2025, the city's cultural calendar is as dynamic and inclusive as ever.

Brighton Festival

Each May, Brighton transforms into one sprawling, sparkling arts venue during the Brighton Festival, now in its 59th year and still gloriously unconventional. Founded in 1967, the festival has evolved into one of the UK's most significant multi-arts celebrations, featuring international talent and local creatives across theatre, music, dance, film, literature, and visual art.

You might find a contemporary ballet performed in a church crypt, an immersive sound installation in a disused swimming pool, or a spoken word performance spilling into a café at dusk. In 2025, highlights include a community-built art trail through Queen's Park and a performance series led by neurodiverse artists exploring new ways of storytelling.

> **Local Insight:** Don't miss the **Children's Parade** that opens the festival. It's a riot of handmade costumes, drums, and infectious energy—a city-wide smile, if ever there was one.

Brighton Fringe

Running alongside the Brighton Festival is its cheeky, rebellious cousin—the Brighton Fringe. It's where emerging talent dares to dream loud and weird. In converted pubs, pop-up theatres, parks, and even laundromats, you'll discover comedy, cabaret, performance art, and just about anything else you didn't know you needed.

It's delightfully unpredictable. One night, you might see a queer reimagining of Shakespeare performed on roller skates; the next, you're at a midnight magic show in a tent behind a noodle bar.

> **Pro Tip:** Buy a multi-show pass and leave a few nights open. Let spontaneity guide you—you never know which obscure act might become your favorite story of the trip.

Pride in Brighton

If there's one event that defines Brighton's spirit, it's **Brighton & Hove Pride**. Held every August, Pride is not only the UK's biggest LGBTQ+ celebration but a vibrant affirmation of love, rights, visibility, and unity. It's a citywide festival that welcomes everyone, whether you're here to march, dance, learn, or simply celebrate being human.

The parade flows from Hove Lawns through the city, awash with glitter, flags, feathers, and fierce joy. But Pride is more than just a party—it includes inclusive talks, queer art exhibitions, and community outreach initiatives that continue long after the music fades.

In 2025, the Pride headline concert returns to **Preston Park** with a dazzling line-up of pop icons, drag royalty, and local legends.

> **Insider Tip:** Book accommodation early—Pride weekend is one of Brighton's busiest times, and hotels fill up fast. Don't forget to explore satellite events like **Queer Takeover** in Kemptown and inclusive film nights at the **Duke of York's Picturehouse**.

Cultural Beacons
The Spaces That Tell Brighton's Stories. Between the big events, Brighton's cultural heartbeat continues in the institutions and grassroots spaces that make this city a year-round creative haven.

Start with the **Brighton Dome**, a stunning Regency-era building that has hosted everything from ABBA's Eurovision win to TEDx talks and classical symphonies. Just next door, the **Brighton Museum & Art Gallery** weaves together the city's history with engaging exhibitions—from the city's rebellious punk roots to immersive digital art installations.

For something more offbeat, head to **ONCA Gallery**, an arts charity focused on environmental and social justice. In 2025, its exhibitions include youth-led climate art projects and a participatory installation exploring migration stories through textiles.

> **Warm Tip:** Many galleries run "pay what you can" entry models or host free artist talks—perfect for both your curiosity and your wallet.

Brighton Digital Festival

Tech Meets Imagination. Held in October, Brighton Digital Festival merges Brighton's creative soul with its growing tech innovation scene. Expect everything from AI-generated poetry readings to augmented reality street art and interactive digital storytelling workshops.

In 2025, the festival's theme **"Play/Power"** invites visitors to explore how technology reshapes identity, culture, and community. You'll find code-meets-art workshops, virtual-reality exhibitions, and discussions led by digital activists and artists alike.

> **Smart Suggestion:** Many events take place at **The FuseBox**, Brighton's hub for digital innovation near the train station. It's worth

popping in to check their rolling calendar, even outside of festival season.

Music, Always

From Backroom Gigs to Beachfront Anthems. Brighton's music scene is ever-alive. Any night of the week, you can catch a punk band blasting in a basement, a jazz trio warming a pub snug, or a world-class DJ spinning under disco balls at **Patterns** or **The Arch**.

In 2025, the **Great Escape Festival** continues to be a pilgrimage for new music lovers. It turns Brighton into a multi-venue showcase for rising stars, with hundreds of acts performing across the city in just a few days. It's where tomorrow's headliners get their start.

> **Personal Pick: Komedia** on Gardner Street is the city's comedy and music cornerstone—book ahead for their legendary **Krater Comedy Club**, or drop in for a genre-bending music night in the downstairs venue.

Brighton's culture isn't confined to a calendar. It's baked into the rhythm of daily life—the street art on the side of a fish n' chip shop, the poetry chalked on pavement slabs, the drag queen reading stories at the local library, or the circus troupe rehearsing in the park.

In this city, you're not just a visitor—you're invited to join in. Paint, perform, parade, participate. The doors are open, the lights are on, and the city is singing. Brighton in 2025 is more than a cultural destination—it's a celebration of self-expression, in every form.

So come curious, leave inspired—and maybe, just maybe, a little more yourself.

Outdoor Adventures & Nature Escapes

Brighton isn't just a city—it's a playground. A wide-open invitation to breathe deeply, move freely, and let nature restore you. Whether you're chasing sunrise over the English Channel, cycling along coastal clifftops, or getting gloriously muddy in the South Downs, Brighton's outdoor adventures are as diverse as its people. And in 2025, the city has never been more in sync with the rhythm of the natural world.

Get ready to lace up your boots, zip your jacket, or maybe kick off your shoes entirely—Brighton's great outdoors is calling.

Beach Days and Beyond
The Iconic Seafront Reimagined. Brighton's legendary pebble beach is the city's beating heart, but in 2025, it's more than just a sunbathing spot—it's a hub for active coastal living.

Start your day with a bracing morning dip—a ritual among Brightonians that's as much about mental clarity as it is cold water courage.

The Brighton Sea Swimmers meet daily near the West Pier ruins. No wetsuit? No worries. They'll welcome you with laughter, warm tea, and plenty of encouragement.

For a new perspective, try stand-up paddleboarding (SUP) or coastal kayaking with Lagoon Watersports at Hove Lagoon. You'll glide past historic piers and maybe even spot a curious seal if you're lucky.

> **Local Tip:** For fewer crowds and a golden glow, head to **Saltdean Beach** in the late afternoon. It's a quiet gem east of Brighton with a gentle slope into the sea and dramatic white cliffs behind you—perfect for sunset picnics.

Hiking the South Downs
Green Adventures at Your Doorstep. Just 15 minutes inland, the cityscape gives way to the undulating beauty of the South Downs National Park, and trust us—this is where Brighton's adventurous soul truly stretches its legs.

A local favorite is the hike from **Devil's Dyke**—a dramatic V-shaped valley carved by Ice Age meltwater. At the top, the views roll endlessly over patchwork fields and villages, and on a clear day, you can see all the way to the Isle of Wight.

Follow the **South Downs Way**, a long-distance path that weaves through chalk hills, ancient woodlands, and sleepy hamlets. Even a few hours on the trail offers wildflowers underfoot and skylarks overhead.

> **Inspiring Option:** Rent an e-bike from Brighton Bike Tours and ride the scenic path from **Preston Park** to **Ditchling Beacon**. It's a workout, but the panoramas at the top are worth every pedal push.

Stanmer Park
A place Where Wilderness Meets Community. Nestled between Brighton and the Downs, **Stanmer Park** is a nature-lover's dream. In 2025, it's buzzing with energy thanks to the newly revitalized **One Garden Brighton**—a horticultural haven where you can wander through themed gardens, grab local produce, or join a foraging workshop.

But the real magic is in the woods. Take the winding paths into the forest and find secret glades perfect for meditating, journaling, or simply losing track of time. On weekends, you might stumble upon a forest yoga class or a community drum circle by the eco-village.

> **Family-Friendly Highlight:** Don't miss the **Stanmer Park Nature Trail**, a gentle 2-mile loop with interactive signs and wildlife-spotting activities for kids—and big kids at heart.

Birdsong and Biodiversity

Nature in Brighton isn't confined to parks—it's woven into the edges, the wild corners that thrive just outside the bustle. For a serene escape, head to the **Wild Park Local Nature Reserve**, a lesser-known sanctuary just north of the city centre. Here, ancient woodland, open meadows, and chalk grasslands host everything from rare orchids to barn owls.

In spring, the area bursts into bloom. In summer, it hums with bees. Bring binoculars or simply wander the quiet trails and reconnect with nature's subtle rhythms.

> **Secret Corner:** At the top of Wild Park lies a panoramic viewpoint locals lovingly call "Happy Valley." It's a perfect sunrise spot, and

in autumn, the golden light through the oaks is utterly magical.

Urban Green Retreats

Parks, Gardens, and Unexpected Beauty. Even in the heart of the city, Brighton nurtures green oases that invite you to pause and play.

Preston Park, Brighton's largest urban green space, is home to rose gardens, rockeries, and spacious lawns where locals sprawl with books, frisbees, and acoustic guitars. Come for a jog, a picnic, or just to people-watch as skaters flip tricks in the skatepark.

Tucked away nearby, **The Level** offers sculptural water features, sensory gardens, and a community vibe that welcomes all. Further east, **Queen's Park** has a more romantic charm—think weeping willows, duck ponds, and old stone walls that beg to be leaned against with a coffee in hand.

> **Hidden Gem:** Seek out **St. Ann's Well Gardens** in Hove. Once famed for its mineral springs, it's now a peaceful park with tree-lined paths, hidden nooks, and friendly squirrels.

Adventure with a Purpose

Brighton's love for the environment isn't just scenic—it's active and hands-on. Eco-tourism is booming in 2025, with a rise in volunteer-led clean-ups, beachcombing education walks, and rewilding projects.

Join a beach clean with Leave No Trace Brighton, or participate in a "citizen science" butterfly survey through the Sussex Wildlife Trust. These experiences offer more than just good vibes—they connect you to Brighton's deep-rooted ethos of environmental care and community spirit.

> **Feeling Inspired?** Look up seasonal volunteering programs through **Brighton Permaculture Trust**, where you can help plant orchards or maintain forest gardens while learning sustainable practices from local experts.

In Brighton, the line between city and wilderness is deliciously blurred. One moment you're sipping a flat white in the Lanes, the next you're standing on a wind-swept cliff, heart pounding, hair tangled by salt and sky. It's this blend of energy and escape, movement and meaning, that makes Brighton's outdoor scene so special.

So don't just pass through. Stretch. Climb. Paddle. Pause. Let the land beneath your feet and the sea at your back remind you what it feels like to be fully alive.

Brighton's nature isn't just scenery—it's your invitation to adventure.

Brighton with Kids

If you're traveling to Brighton with children in tow, take a deep breath—you're in just the right place. Brighton is a city that wears its child-friendly credentials proudly and without fuss. There's something wonderfully freeing about being here with kids. It's the sort of place where puddle-jumping on the promenade is totally acceptable, seagull-spotting counts as entertainment, and ice cream before lunch isn't just allowed—it's encouraged.

In 2025, Brighton continues to balance old-school seaside fun with imaginative, inclusive activities that make families feel both welcome and excited. Whether you're navigating toddler meltdowns or entertaining curious teens, Brighton offers relaxed rhythms and playful surprises for all ages.

Classic Seaside Fun
Brighton Palace Pier & Beachfront Play
Let's start with the obvious: Brighton Palace Pier is a hit with kids of all ages. Step onto this candy-striped wonderland and it's like entering a time capsule of seaside joy. Arcade games blink and beep, candyfloss floats through the

air, and carousel horses glimmer in the salty breeze.

In 2025, the Pier's small rides and attractions will see thoughtful upgrades—safety, accessibility, and clean facilities are top priorities now. There's a designated **Toddler Zone** for little ones and newer eco-conscious food vendors that cater to picky eaters and plant-based families alike.

The adjacent **Volk's Electric Railway**, Britain's oldest operating electric railway, still charms kids with its pint-sized trains and seaside views. It runs from the Pier to **Black Rock**, where you'll find the newer **Beach Box Sauna Village**—not necessarily for kids, but a great place for grown-ups to take turns recharging while the other parent tackles sandcastle duty!

> **Parent Tip:** Brighton's beach is pebbly, so bring sturdy sandals or water shoes. The tide pools at **Ovingdean Beach**, just east of the city, are a quieter alternative for curious explorers.

Playgrounds & Parks

Space to Run and Roam. When it's time to let the kids blow off steam, Brighton delivers in a green and playful style.

Queen's Park is a family favorite, tucked in a leafy pocket of the city with an excellent enclosed playground, a duck pond, and open lawns for football or kite-flying. It's stroller-friendly and often dotted with local families—expect to make a friend or two.

For something more energetic, **The Level** offers a modern adventure playground with climbing frames, water features, and a skatepark that's always buzzing with tweens trying out new tricks. Grab a coffee from the community café and relax under one of the shady trees while the kids run wild.

Don't miss **Preston Park**, Brighton's largest green space, with a rock garden and mini maze, or **Hove Park**, home to a miniature railway that runs on weekends—a total thrill for little train lovers.

Museums, Curiosities, and Rainy-Day Wonders Brighton's not just a fair-weather city. When clouds roll in or attention spans waver, there are plenty of indoor spots that mix learning with fun.

Brighton Toy and Model Museum, tucked under Brighton Station, is a treasure trove of nostalgia and wonder. Imagine shelves stacked with vintage dolls, antique train sets, and mechanical toys that make adults wistful and kids wide-eyed.

For hands-on fun, **SEA LIFE Brighton** remains a firm favorite. The Victorian-era aquarium has undergone a 21st-century transformation, now featuring immersive displays, interactive zones, and a walk-through ocean tunnel where sharks and rays glide overhead. It's educational and genuinely thrilling.

Nearby, the **Brighton Museum & Art Gallery** in the Royal Pavilion Gardens has a "Family Discovery Zone" updated in 2025 with sensory-friendly exhibits and child-focused storytelling sessions—perfect for quieter moments.

> **Rainy Day Hack:** Drop into **Jubilee Library**—Brighton's central library has a beautiful kids' section with beanbags, story

times, and local families looking to escape the drizzle just like you.

Seaside Treats & Kid-Friendly Eats

Hungry kids (and parents) are no joke. Thankfully, Brighton's food scene caters beautifully to young palates and grown-up taste buds alike.

Grab an easy picnic from **Infinity Foods** (think fresh bread, fruit, and homemade treats), or pick up freshly made fish and chips from **Bardsley's**—a local institution since the 1920s and now offering grilled and gluten-free options.

For indoor family dining, **Fatto a Mano** is a pizza place that strikes the perfect balance between casual and cool. Kids love watching their pizzas go into the flaming oven, and parents love the Negroni on tap.

Craving something sweet? Brighton's **Gelato Gusto** on Gardner Street has inventive flavors (peanut butter & jelly, anyone?) and friendly service that keeps kids smiling. For an allergy-conscious option, **Cloud 9** in the North Laine offers dairy-free, gluten-free cupcakes and marshmallow treats that don't compromise on taste.

> **Snack Smart:** Many Brighton cafes now have toy baskets, coloring sheets, and baby-changing facilities—a sign of how family-friendly this city has become.

Want something a little different? Hop on a bus to **Stanmer Park**, just outside the city. There's a woodland adventure trail, a walled garden to explore, and even kid-friendly workshops on weekends—from apple pressing to bug hunting.

Or catch the breeze with a cycle ride along the **Undercliff Path**, a safe, flat route that stretches from the Marina to Saltdean. Stop along the way to hunt for fossils in chalky rock formations or have a seaside picnic on grassy terraces.

What makes Brighton with kids so delightful isn't just the activities—it's the atmosphere. It's a city that doesn't just tolerate families; it embraces them. Children are visible and valued here. You'll find ramps where you need them, cafés that don't mind strollers, and smiling locals happy to offer directions—or a spare beach toy.

Whether you're here for a weekend or staying the whole summer, Brighton gently encourages you to slow down, tune in, and enjoy the beauty of family life with the sea as your soundtrack.

So grab your buckets, bring your sense of wonder, and dive into a city that knows how to make childhood—and parenting—a little more magical.

Accommodation in Brighton

Where You Stay Shapes How You Feel

Finding the right place to stay can be the difference between a good trip and a great one—and in Brighton, your options are as varied and vibrant as the city itself. Whether you're here for a romantic weekend, a solo soul-search, a family beach holiday, or a creative sabbatical, Brighton welcomes you with places to rest that reflect its character: friendly, independent, stylish, and a little unconventional.

As of 2025, the city has thoughtfully adapted to the needs of modern travelers. You'll find high-speed Wi-Fi is a given, accessibility features are taken seriously, and sustainable practices are increasingly part of the hospitality DNA. From boutique townhouses to seafront hotels, cozy B\& Bs to self-catering apartments in quirky neighborhoods, there's a space in Brighton waiting to become your home away from home.

Seafront Charm

Stay with a View. If waking up to the sound of waves is your dream, Brighton's seafront hotels make it a reality. Stretching from the bustling Brighton Palace Pier westward past the i360 observation tower, the promenade is dotted with historic buildings now reborn as elegant hotels.

One standout is **The Grand Brighton**, a regal 19th-century hotel with sweeping staircases, chandeliers, and sea views that inspire poetry. In 2025, it continues to marry old-world charm with contemporary service and eco-conscious updates—think solar panels, refillable toiletries, and locally sourced breakfast menus.

Just a few doors down, **Drakes of Brighton** offers a more intimate, design-forward experience. Known for its freestanding bathtubs facing the ocean and discreet luxury, it's ideal for couples seeking a romantic retreat.

If you prefer a modern, more budget-conscious seafront option, **Selina Brighton** is a community-driven hotel-hostel hybrid with a creative edge. It caters to digital nomads, solo travelers, and backpackers, offering coworking spaces, yoga classes, and a rooftop café with incredible sunsets over the Channel.

> **Traveler Tip:** Book early if you're visiting during Brighton Festival (May) or Pride (August). Prices and availability shift fast!

North Laine & The Lanes

Quirky, Central, and Full of Character, For those who want to be close to the action, Brighton's heart beats strongest in **North Laine** and **The Lanes**—two neighboring areas that hum with life, indie spirit, and color.

Artist Residence Brighton, nestled between the two districts, feels more like staying in a friend's curated loft than a hotel. Each room is uniquely decorated, often by local artists, and there's a rooftop bar and café that spills out onto Regency Square. It's popular with creatives, couples, and even small families who want to stay somewhere truly memorable.

In The Lanes, you'll find charming B\&Bs like **Hotel du Vin**, offering vintage elegance with a twist. Think wine-inspired rooms, roll-top tubs, and a courtyard bistro that's a favorite among locals and guests alike.

Airbnb and serviced apartments are also plentiful in these neighborhoods. If you're staying for more than a few nights, a self-catering flat in the North Laine puts you steps from street performers, thrift stores, and some of the city's best brunch spots.

> **Supportive Suggestion:** These areas can get lively at night. If you're traveling with young children or light sleepers, request a room away from the street or opt for quieter neighborhoods like Hove.

Hove
Sophisticated Calm with a Local Feel. Right in the West of central Brighton lies **Hove**, Brighton's calmer cousin. It's still coastal, still stylish, but with a more residential rhythm that appeals to families, long-stay travelers, and anyone craving a little more space.

Hove's iconic **Brunswick Square** and **Palmeira Avenue** are dotted with elegant Victorian townhouses, many converted into guesthouses or boutique apartments. **The Claremont** is a serene B\&B with a garden perfect for morning tea or reading sessions, while **Sea Spray Suites** offer sleek self-catering flats ideal for longer visits.

Hove's seafront is quieter and more relaxed, with broad beaches and playgrounds, and you're never far from independent bakeries, kid-friendly cafés, and lush green spaces like **St. Ann's Well Gardens.**

> **Insider Insight:** Hove doesn't have the nightlife buzz of central Brighton—which might be exactly what makes it perfect for restful evenings.

Budget-Friendly Stays
Traveling on a budget in Brighton doesn't mean compromising on comfort or character. In 2025, the city has embraced the rise of affordable boutique hotels and ethical hostels.

YHA Brighton, housed in a historic Regency building just minutes from the beach, continues to be a great choice for families, groups, and solo travelers. Rooms are clean and modern, with private options available, and there's a communal kitchen and regular social events.

Kipps Brighton and **Backpackers Hostel** in the North Laine area attract young travelers and students with friendly vibes and prices to match. These places offer not just a bed but a community—a great way to meet fellow adventurers.

For ultra-budget travelers, local platforms often list short-term room rentals in shared homes. Just ensure your accommodation is registered with Brighton & Hove City Council, as the city keeps a close eye on legal and ethical short lets.

Sustainable Stays

Sustainability is more than a buzzword in Brighton. Many accommodation providers now prioritize eco-conscious practices—from low-energy systems and zero-plastic policies to sourcing local produce and minimizing waste.

One Broad Street, a smart, minimalist boutique hotel near the seafront, offers a tech-savvy stay with a low carbon footprint. There's no front desk—check-in is app-based—but each room is thoughtfully stocked with local products and environmentally friendly amenities.

More properties are also participating in the **Green Tourism Business Scheme**, so keep an eye out for those badges when you book. It's an easy way to ensure your stay supports the city's commitment to green living.

At the end of the day, your Brighton accommodation should reflect your pace, your people, and your purpose. Whether you're here to unwind, explore, or be inspired, there's a room—or flat or bunk or townhouse—ready to welcome you.

Trust that wherever you stay, the spirit of Brighton—welcoming, eclectic, and beautifully human—will meet you at the door.

Local Flavours and Must-Try Dishes

A Feast for the Senses by the Sea

Brighton isn't just a city that you see, hear, and feel—it's one you taste. Every bite here tells a story, whether it's whispered from a fisherman's boat anchored off the coast or baked slowly in the oven of an old corner café. Brighton's food scene is playful, progressive, and deeply proud of its local roots. In 2025, the city remains a paradise for food lovers: from street eats and seaside classics to globally inspired vegan dishes, there's always something simmering that will tempt you to stay just a little longer.

Seaside Staples

Let's start at the edge of the sea, where Brighton's most iconic dish—**fish** and **chips**—still reigns supreme. But don't expect a soggy paper-wrapped mess. In 2025, Brighton's chippies have elevated this seaside staple to an art form.

Bardsley's of Baker Street, a family-run institution, serves golden battered cod with chunky chips and a perfect balance of crispy and flaky. It's the kind of place where the vinegar is liberally poured and the tartar sauce is made fresh in-house. Sit down, slow down, and savor the old-school charm.

For a modern twist, try **Little Fish Market** in Hove. Here, the catch of the day is treated with reverence—pan-seared bream, line-caught mackerel, or sustainably farmed trout are often served with foraged herbs and seasonal vegetables. It's seafood with a story.

> **Local Tip:** If you're strolling the pier, grab a cone of calamari or scampi from the food stalls near the carousel. The sea breeze adds an extra layer of seasoning.

Plant-Powered Paradise
Brighton has long been a leader in plant-based dining, and in 2025, it continues to shine as one of the UK's most vegan-friendly cities. You don't have to be a full-time herbivore to fall in love with what's on offer.

Food for Friends, tucked into a quiet lane just off The Lanes, is a Brighton institution. Their miso-glazed aubergine with black rice is deeply umami-rich, and the wild mushroom arancini is a crunchy, creamy dream.

Meanwhile, **Terre à Terre**, known for its daring flavor combinations and globally inspired menu, dazzles with dishes like tamarind-glazed tofu with Szechuan greens and wasabi tempura.

Craving fast food with a conscience? **Vurger Co.** and **Neon Vegan Diner** on London Road serve plant-based burgers, loaded fries, and shakes that could convert even the staunchest meat-eater. Think stacked beetroot patties, house-made sauces, and fries dusted with seaweed salt.

> **Traveler Insight:** Most restaurants now clearly label vegan, vegetarian, and gluten-free options. Many even source ingredients from within Sussex to keep things fresh and eco-friendly.

Sweet Treats & Afternoon Indulgences
No trip to Brighton is complete without something sweet, and this city knows how to treat your taste buds.

Begin with a **Brighton rock**—a classic peppermint candy stick that still evokes childhood memories and souvenir shops by the sea. You'll find them in all colors and flavors, often spelling out the word "Brighton" right through the center.

But for something more refined, make your way to **Julien Plumart**, an elegant patisserie near the Royal Pavilion. Here, jewel-toned macarons and delicate tartlets compete with buttery croissants and the richest hot chocolate in town.

Afternoon tea, of course, is a Brighton ritual. At **The Ivy in The Lanes**, indulge in finger sandwiches, scones with clotted cream and jam, and dainty cakes served under chandeliers with a touch of vintage glamour. Or, for a cozy, less formal experience, **Black Mocha** offers specialty coffee, artisan cakes, and a signature chocolate mocha that locals swear by.

> **Reassuring Note:** Traveling with dietary restrictions? Brighton's cafés and bakeries are remarkably inclusive—just ask, and they'll likely have a dairy-free, nut-free, or low-sugar alternative ready.

World on a Plate
Thanks to its diverse population and welcoming spirit, Brighton offers an international dining scene that spans

continents while staying true to its own character.

In **Kemptown**, you'll find **Moshimo**, a Japanese sushi bar with sustainable credentials and a rooftop garden. Their vegan sushi platter—featuring pickled radish, avocado, beetroot, and tofu—is as vibrant as a Brighton sunset.

Head to **Befries** on West Street for a taste of Belgian-style double-cooked chips with a mind-boggling array of sauces, or drop into **Curry Leaf Café** for South Indian street food—dosas, coconut curries, and saffron rice in a warm, spice-scented atmosphere.

Craving Middle Eastern flavors? **Schmorl's** in Brighton Open Market is famous for its handmade hummus bowls, grilled falafel, and fluffy pita straight from the oven.

> **Cultural Connection:** Many of these independent eateries double as community hubs, hosting music nights, poetry readings, or art exhibitions. Dining out in Brighton is often a full sensory experience.

Markets & Artisan Bites: For a true Brighton experience, eat like a local—and that often means grazing your way through one of its bustling markets.

Brighton Open Market on London Road is a treasure trove of artisanal goods: handmade cheeses, organic breads, wildflower honey, and hot food from around the world. On weekends, the **Brighton Farmers' Market** in Hove features fresh Sussex produce, from heritage tomatoes and just-picked asparagus to gourmet chutneys and cider.

Don't miss **Flour Pot Bakery**, with locations across the city. Their sourdough, cinnamon buns, and sausage rolls (including vegan versions) are beloved by locals. Grab a loaf and picnic at **Queen's Park** or the seaside lawns of Hove.

In Brighton, food is more than sustenance—it's a celebration of creativity, culture, and community. Whether you're tucking into a hand-wrapped falafel on the beach or lingering over sea bass at a fine dining bistro, every meal adds another layer to your adventure.

So loosen your belt, follow your nose, and let your appetite lead the way. Brighton is ready to serve up memories, one delicious bite at a time.

Where to Eat and Drink

A City with a Passion for Food and a Love of Libation

Brighton has always worn its heart on its sleeve, and in 2025, that heart beats strongest in its pubs, restaurants, cafés, and cocktail bars. Whether you're grabbing a beachside bite, sipping a flat white in a leafy square, or discovering a candlelit wine bar down a quiet lane, eating and drinking here feels less like a transaction and more like a warm invitation.

One of the best things about Brighton's food and drink scene? It's refreshingly unpretentious. The focus is on quality, personality, and creativity—served without fuss. The city also champions independent businesses, so many of the best places are small, owner-run spots that truly care about what they serve.

Let's explore where you can eat well and drink happily across this vibrant coastal city.

Breakfast and Brunch

The Most Important Meal of the Day (Especially in Brighton . Brightonians don't just brunch—they elevate it to a lifestyle. On weekends, you'll see queues forming outside cafés as locals settle in for long, lazy mornings over sourdough toast and specialty coffee.

Start your day at **Starfish & Coffee**, tucked just behind Queen's Park. This cozy, welcoming café is known for its fluffy pancakes, eggs Benedict variations, and a community feel that makes solo diners feel right at home.

Over in **Seven Dials**, **The Flour Pot Bakery** has expanded its breakfast menu to include brioche breakfast buns, avocado-topped toast with za'atar, and divine cinnamon swirls. Grab a seat outside if the weather is fair, and soak up the buzz of one of Brighton's leafiest neighborhoods.

If you're looking for something health-conscious and plant-based, **Oeuf** in Hove blends style and substance. Think smashed peas with lemon ricotta, vibrant smoothie bowls, and turmeric lattes served in pastel ceramic cups.

> **Honest Tip:** Brighton cafés can get crowded after 10am on weekends. Arrive early or plan a weekday brunch to avoid the lines.

Lunch Spots with Character and Charm

Brighton excels at casual, mid-day dining. Whether you want something quick or you're ready to linger, you'll find plenty of places with personality.

Foodilic on North Street offers an all-you-can-eat buffet that's affordable and packed with colorful salads, hot curries, and roasted vegetable dishes. It's a hit with students, creatives, and anyone who loves a filling, healthy plate without a heavy price tag.

Over near the seafront, **Riddle & Finns** is a hidden gem. The original oyster bar on Meeting House Lane serves fresh seafood in a candlelit, marble-clad setting—perfect for a slightly indulgent lunch. Their clam chowder and crab linguine are especially popular.

For a taste of Brighton's eclectic side, visit **The Pond** on Gloucester Road. By day, it's a relaxed pub with craft beers and incredible Taiwanese street food (courtesy of resident kitchen **Baby Bao**). Their gua bao buns—pillowy, packed with flavor, and dripping with hoisin sauce—are worth the sticky fingers.

Dinner Destinations for Every Mood

Whether you're looking for romance, atmosphere, or just something hearty and delicious, Brighton delivers on dinner.

Etch., led by MasterChef: The Professionals winner Steven Edwards, offers a seasonal tasting menu that showcases local produce with finesse. It's not cheap, but if you're celebrating something special, it's an experience worth the splurge.

For a more laid-back but equally impressive meal, **Cin Cin** serves Italian small plates in a stylish but friendly space. The pasta is handmade daily, the service is warm, and the negronis are strong.

Families or groups might feel more at home at **Fatto a Mano**, Brighton's beloved Neapolitan pizza joint with locations in North Laine and Hove. The pizzas are wood-fired, simple, and addictive—especially the nduja and burrata.

Looking for something different? **Pompoko**, just up from the Royal Pavilion, offers fast and affordable Japanese rice bowls and noodle dishes. It's a student favorite for good reason:

the food is quick, satisfying, and surprisingly tasty for the price.

Where to Drink

Drinking in Brighton is about the atmosphere. Each pub, bar, or café tells a different story, from historic haunts to modern mixology.

Start with a classic: The Basketmakers Arms in North Laine. It's cozy, unpretentious, and full of character. You'll find a rotating selection of ales, classic pub food, and handwritten notes stuffed into old tins on the wall—curious, charming, and uniquely Brighton.

If craft beer is your thing, **The Brighton Beer Dispensary** on Dean Street features small-batch brews from Sussex and beyond. Try anything by **UnBarred Brewery**—a local favorite known for experimental flavors like mango pale ale and milk stout.

For cocktails, **GungHo!** on Preston Street leads the way in sustainable mixology. The menu changes seasonally, with drinks made from foraged herbs, local spirits, and house-fermented ingredients. It's a small, low-lit spot—ideal for a quiet drink or a date night.

Prefer a low-key coffee or tea? **Pelicano** is a local indie coffee roaster with serious passion. Their two Brighton cafés serve excellent pour-overs and pastries, making them perfect for a midday recharge. And for tea lovers, **Bluebird Tea Co**. offers a dazzling range of creative blends like strawberry lemonade or rooibos chai.

> **Helpful Note:** Many of Brighton's pubs and cafés double as event spaces. Check chalkboards or websites for open mic nights, comedy shows, or DJ sets. You might just stumble into something memorable.

Brighton isn't about fine-dining pageantry or over-the-top trends. It's about people—chefs, baristas, bakers, and brewers—who love what they do and want to share it with you. You'll find food here that comforts, excites, surprises, and satisfies.

So whether you're eating a seaside lunch with the salt in your hair, sipping something strange and delightful at a cocktail bar, or devouring a slice of pizza under fairy lights, you'll quickly understand why Brighton's food and drink scene is as much about the mood as the menu.

Bring your curiosity, your appetite, and maybe a reusable water bottle—and let Brighton feed you.

Foodie Activities and Tastings

If there's one thing Brighton knows how to do brilliantly, it's making food fun. In 2025, this vibrant coastal city is not just about **what** you eat but **how** you experience it. Whether you're dunking a freshly fried doughnut at a local market, stirring saffron into a paella during a hands-on cooking class, or hopping from stall to stall on a curated food tour, Brighton offers countless ways to dive headfirst into its buzzing food culture.

This chapter is your guide to the most mouthwatering, interactive, and unforgettable foodie activities around Brighton. It's time to roll up your sleeves, grab your fork (or chopsticks), and get stuck in.

Brighton Food Tours

Let's start with a must-do experience for any culinary adventurer: the legendary **Brighton Food Tours.** These guided walking tours weave through the North Laine and Lanes districts, introducing you to Brighton's best-kept secrets—from micro-bakeries tucked behind record shops to vegan chocolate makers crafting magic in small-batch kitchens.

The "**VIB Tour**" (Very Independent Brighton) is especially popular. You'll sample at least six different treats—think artisanal cheese, freshly made falafel, local wine, and even Sussex-made gin—while meeting the passionate producers behind the products. The guides are Brighton locals who bring humour, history, and insider tips to every bite.

> **Insider Tip:** Book early—these tours are capped at small groups for a more intimate (and tasty) experience. Also, come hungry!

Cooking Classes

There's something deeply satisfying about learning to cook a dish and then devouring it. Brighton offers a smorgasbord of culinary classes for all skill levels—perfect for solo travelers, couples, or families looking for something unique and enriching.

Head to **Community Kitchen Brighton**, a social enterprise space just off Queens Road. Their lineup in 2025 includes Indian street food nights, Thai curry workshops, and plant-based baking sessions, all led by local chefs who bring warmth and storytelling to every lesson. You'll chop, stir, and laugh your way to a delicious shared meal.

Craving something Mediterranean? **Mange Tout**, the beloved French café on Trafalgar Street, now runs evening bread-making workshops in its cozy kitchen. Learn how to shape baguettes, knead sourdough, and even tackle the elusive croissant—all with a glass of natural wine in hand.

Artisan Tastings

If your ideal afternoon includes shipping, swirling, and nibbling in good company, Brighton delivers. The city's appreciation for artisanal craftsmanship runs deep, and tasting sessions are the perfect way to savor the results.

Start at **Brighton's Cheese Shop** in the Open Market. This little slice of dairy heaven showcases local favourites like Sussex Brie and Brighton Blue, as well as curated European classics. On weekends, they host intimate tasting flights with chutneys, crackers, and a splash of cider or ale to complement the cheese.

For something a little stronger, venture to **Brighton Gin Distillery** in the Portslade area. This cheerful, LGBTQ+ founded distillery is a Brighton icon, and their tasting tours are equal parts educational and intoxicating. You'll learn about their eco-conscious distilling process (they reuse and hand-label every bottle), sample limited-edition gins, and maybe even bottle your own.

Wine lovers shouldn't miss **Vine & Dine**, a chic wine bar in Hove that runs weekend tasting experiences featuring Sussex's growing wine scene. In 2025, local vineyards like Rathfinny and Albourne Estate are producing award-winning sparkling wines that rival Champagne—and this is the best place to try them without leaving the city.

Markets and Pop-Ups
Brighton's markets are not just places to shop—they're places to taste, discover, and connect. Every corner hums with aromas and colors, offering a bite-sized journey through global cuisines.

The **Brighton Open Market** (off London Road) is a food lover's playground. Sample kimchi fries from a Korean fusion stall, sip

Moroccan mint tea, or grab a spinach and feta börek from the Turkish baker on the corner. On Saturdays, the market often features live music, giving your foodie exploration a lively soundtrack.

For street food, head to **Shelter Hall** on the seafront. Housed in a grand Victorian building, it's a modern food court done right. You'll find rotating kitchen residencies here—2025's line-up includes spicy Sri Lankan curries, artisanal tacos, and vegan doughnuts filled with cardamom custard. Grab a table with a sea view, and watch the sun dip behind the pier as you feast.

> **Excited Explorer's Tip:** Many of Brighton's best food experiences are seasonal. Keep an eye on local listings or Instagram to find special pop-up nights, rooftop supper clubs, or beach barbecues hosted by local chefs.

No foodie adventure is complete without a sugar fix. Brighton's sweet scene is as playful and inventive as the city itself.

Drop by **Boho Gelato**, just steps from the seafront, for unusual and delicious handmade ice cream. Their 2025 flavors range from

Brighton Rock ripple to vegan chocolate and orange zest—rotated weekly so there's always something new.

If baked goods are more your style, **Julien Plumart** on Queens Road is a decadent little haven of French patisserie. Rows of vibrant macarons, flaky mille-feuilles, and raspberry éclairs are displayed like jewelry—too pretty to eat but too tempting to resist.

And for pure nostalgic joy, **Dough Lover**, a new star in the Brighton dessert scene, offers hot, gooey cookie dough bowls with toppings like marshmallow fluff, salted caramel, and crushed pretzels. Late-night indulgence?

Brighton's foodie soul is alive, welcoming, and full of surprises. This city doesn't just feed you—it invites you into its kitchens, markets, and stories. Whether you're nibbling your way through a guided tour, getting flour-dusted in a baking class, or sipping Sussex wine as seagulls wheel overhead, every moment offers a delicious way to connect more deeply with the place and its people.

So go ahead: follow your nose, say yes to the next bite, and let your tastebuds lead the way. Brighton is ready to be tasted.

Where to Shop in Brighton

Brighton has long been a haven for shoppers craving a dose of individuality, creativity, and charm — and in 2025, it's more vibrant than ever. Whether you're hunting for quirky vintage finds, cutting-edge fashion, or artisan crafts with a local story, Brighton's eclectic neighborhoods serve up a treasure trove of retail delights. Here, shopping isn't just about ticking boxes — it's a joyful adventure wrapped in history, culture, and coastal breezes.

So, grab your tote bag (eco-friendly, of course), slip on your comfiest shoes, and get ready to explore where Brighton's best shopping spots come alive.

North Laine

Start your retail journey in **North Laine**, the beating indie heart of the city. This bohemian quarter feels like a bustling village where colorful shop fronts spill onto cobbled streets and the air hums with creativity.

In 2025, North Laine continues to thrive as a hub for independent boutiques, vintage havens, and art galleries. You'll find **Nelly Duff**, an iconic gallery-meets-store, showcasing quirky prints and books by Brighton's flourishing artists. Don't miss **Flagship Vintage**, where racks of curated retro clothing span decades, perfect for those who love a little nostalgic flair mixed with modern style.

The area's charm lies in its delightful unpredictability: one day you might stumble upon a popup shop selling handmade ceramics, the next a vibrant street market bursting with handmade jewelry and ethically sourced goods. Locals and visitors alike treasure North Laine for its friendly, personal service and the chance to discover truly one-of-a-kind pieces.

> **Local Tip:** Stop by **Coffee\@33** between shops for a quality flat white — it's the perfect pick-me-up in a cozy space adorned with local art.

The Lanes

Just a short stroll from North Laine, The Lanes offer a contrasting shopping experience steeped in history and elegance. These winding narrow alleyways, dating back to the 14th century, are home to a curated mix of stylish boutiques, artisanal jewelers, and high-end independent stores that have embraced Brighton's coastal cool.

In 2025, The Lanes are particularly popular for bespoke jewelry and luxury gifts. **Tatty Devine, Brighton's** beloved statement jewelry designer, continues to delight with their vibrant, playful pieces crafted with love and a dash of cheekiness. Nearby, the Brighton Toy and Model Museum Shop offers a nostalgic touch for collectors and children alike, blending history with whimsy.

For fashion lovers, The Lanes also feature emerging designer shops championing sustainable fashion — a nod to Brighton's ongoing commitment to eco-conscious shopping. Don't miss **The Chichester's**, a boutique known for its bold, sustainable outerwear that pairs perfectly with the seaside breeze.

Churchill Square and Beyond

If you're craving a more contemporary shopping experience with all your favorite high-street brands under one roof, head to **Churchill Square Shopping Centre**. Fully revamped by 2025, it blends convenience with style, featuring flagship stores alongside independent cafes where you can rest your feet and refuel.

Here you'll find everything from fashion giants like Zara and H\&M to cutting-edge tech stores and Brighton-centric gift shops. The centre regularly hosts local designer pop-ups in its airy atrium, offering a wonderful bridge between big brands and small creators.

Just outside the centre, the **Brighton Marina** adds a nautical flair to your shopping day. With boutiques, homeware stores, and a vibrant farmers market on weekends, it's a stylish spot to grab unique home décor inspired by the sea, plus gourmet food stalls perfect for picnic supplies.

Beyond the Usual
Unique Markets and Hidden Gems

Brighton's true shopping magic often lies off the beaten path. The **Brighton Open Market** on London Road is a bustling hub for artisan foods, crafts, and vintage wares, ideal for picking up handcrafted gifts or indulging in local delicacies.

Every second Sunday, the **Brighton Flea Market** in the New England Quarter bursts to life with antique hunters and collectors. Whether you're after retro vinyl, vintage postcards, or quirky homewares, it's a vibrant experience brimming with character.

For something truly different, explore the **Artists Open Houses Festival** (held annually in May but with year-round studios open around town). This event invites visitors to visit local artists' homes and studios, offering direct access to original artworks, ceramics, and prints—perfect for anyone who wants to bring a bit of Brighton's creativity home.

Shopping with a Conscience
Brighton's Sustainable and Ethical Scene

Brighton proudly leads the way in sustainable shopping, and 2025 is no exception. Many stores here operate on a "shop less, choose well" ethos, encouraging quality over quantity.

Earth Square, a community shop on Edward Street, specializes in zero-waste household goods, organic clothing, and cruelty-free beauty products. Nearby, **Ethical Wares** offers a handpicked collection of fair-trade fashion and homeware, connecting shoppers with makers from across the globe.

Brighton's commitment to ethical shopping also extends to regular events like swap shops and repair cafés, where you can refresh your wardrobe or fix your favorite shoes — a perfect reminder that style can be sustainable and fun.

Final Tips for Stylish Shopping in Brighton
* **Timing is everything:** Weekdays tend to be quieter, but weekends bring markets and pop-ups to life. Arrive early to catch the freshest finds!
* **Pack light and bring a reusable bag:** You'll want to collect treasures, and Brighton loves eco-friendly shoppers.
* **Chat with shop owners:** Brighton retailers are famously friendly and passionate; a quick chat often leads to the best insider tips on what's new and upcoming.

Brighton's shopping scene is a vibrant celebration of individuality, community, and style with a side of coastal charm. Whether you're a vintage treasure hunter, a high-street aficionado, or someone who loves discovering ethical brands, this city invites you to shop with a smile and leave with more than just bags—leave with stories, connections, and maybe a little bit of Brighton magic.

Suggested Itineraries

Brighton is a city that effortlessly blends laid-back seaside charm with vibrant culture and creative spirit. Whether you've got just a few hours or a whole week to explore, Brighton always has a way to make your visit unforgettable. To help you make the most of your time in this sunny South Coast gem, here are some flexible, fun, and thoughtfully curated itineraries tailored to different types of travelers.

No matter your pace or passion, you'll find a path that feels just right — whether you want to immerse yourself in art and history, embrace the outdoors, or simply soak up the city's infectious energy.

One Day in Brighton
For those with only a day to spare, Brighton packs an impressive punch. Start your morning with a stroll along the iconic **Brighton Palace Pier** — the salty air, vintage arcade sounds, and seaside views instantly set the tone for your day. Grab a traditional fish and chips breakfast or a freshly brewed coffee at **The Coal Shed** just off the pier to fuel up.

Next, wander into **The Lanes,** Brighton's historic maze of narrow streets. Here you can browse independent boutiques, artisanal shops, and maybe grab a quick sweet treat at **Choccywoccydoodah**, the city's famous chocolate haven.

By midday, head to the majestic **Royal Pavilion**, the exotic former royal palace with its flamboyant Indo-Saracenic architecture — a true visual feast and a glimpse into Brighton's aristocratic past.

In the afternoon, explore the creative heart of Brighton in **North Laine**, where murals splash color across buildings and quirky stores beckon. If time allows, pop into the **Brighton Museum & Art Gallery** housed in the Pavilion gardens.

Wrap up your day with a leisurely walk or bike ride along the **Undercliff Walk** — a breathtaking cliffside promenade offering sweeping views of the sea, perfect to watch the sunset and feel the sea breeze on your face.

Family-Friendly Brighton
Three Days of Fun for All Ages
Brighton is wonderfully welcoming for families, blending outdoor fun with educational and interactive experiences.

Day One starts at the **Sea Life Brighton Aquarium**, the oldest operating aquarium in the world, where kids (and adults!) can marvel at vibrant marine creatures. Follow this with an afternoon at **Brighton Toy and Model Museum**, a treasure trove of nostalgia and miniature marvels.

On **Day Two,** visit **Pavilion Gardens** and enjoy a picnic amid beautifully landscaped grounds. Nearby, the **Brighton Toy Library** offers playtime sessions and resources if you're traveling with little ones. Then, spend the afternoon at **Brighton Beach**, building sandcastles or renting pedal boats.

Day Three is perfect for a day trip to **Stanmer Park**, a short bus ride from the city center. This expansive green space offers nature trails, a playground, and horse riding lessons. End your trip with an ice cream at one of the cozy cafes lining the beachfront.

The Arts & Culture Explorer
Four Days of Creativity and History

Brighton's creative soul pulses through its galleries, theaters, and historic venues — and four days here gives you a deep dive into its vibrant arts scene.

Begin with a visit to the **Brighton Dome**, a striking arts venue where you can catch live music, theater, and dance. Check their schedule ahead for must-see performances or exhibitions.

Spend your second day in **North Laine** and **The Lanes**, soaking up street art, gallery-hopping, and shopping for prints and handmade crafts. Don't miss **The Fabrica Gallery** for contemporary art exhibitions, or pop into **Green Door Store** for rare vinyl and music memorabilia.

Day three invites you to the **Booth Museum of Natural History**, a quirky and fascinating collection that appeals to both science buffs and art lovers intrigued by natural forms.

On your last day, stroll along the seafront to **Volks Electric Railway** and enjoy a vintage tram ride. End at the **Brighton Fringe**

Festival (if you're visiting in May-June), which showcases cutting-edge local performance art, comedy, and experimental theater.

The Outdoor Adventurer's Four-Day Escape

Brighton's coastal location and lush nearby countryside make it an ideal base for outdoor enthusiasts who want both city buzz and nature's calm.

Start with a morning bike ride along the **Undercliff Walk**, then hike the **South Downs Way** — the rolling chalk hills just beyond Brighton are alive with wildflowers and offer panoramic views of the English Channel.

Day two calls for water sports: try stand-up paddleboarding or sailing at **Brighton Marina**. Local rental shops provide beginner-friendly lessons and gear.

On day three, venture to **Devil's Dyke**, a stunning valley with trails for hiking, paragliding spots, and picnic areas. If you're lucky, you might catch a local festival or open-air yoga session here.

Day four is perfect for a relaxed beach day at **Hove Beach**, followed by exploring the **Brighton Marina's** waterfront shops and eateries. For a grand finale, climb the **British Airways i360** — the soaring observation tower — to catch a bird's-eye view of the city and coastline.

Flexible Tips for Making the Most of Your Time

* **Mix and match!** Don't feel confined by these itineraries. Brighton's neighborhoods are small and walkable, so combining arts with outdoor fun or family activities is a breeze.

* **Local transport** is friendly and frequent: buses, bikes, and even electric scooters make getting around easy and eco-conscious.

* **Eat as you go** — Brighton's café culture means you can snack on locally roasted coffee and fresh pastries anytime, keeping your energy up for exploring.

* **Weather-proof your plans:** Brighton's weather can be changeable, so have indoor options ready, like the museums or quirky shops, especially in cooler months.

Brighton's compact size and rich character mean every visitor can craft a uniquely memorable experience. Whether you're chasing adrenaline, cultural gems, or family-friendly fun, the city's layered charm invites you to discover and rediscover its magic on your own terms.

So, pack a sense of adventure, bring your curiosity, and let Brighton surprise you with its perfect blend of sea, style, and spirited energy!

Brighton Essentials

Brighton is one of the UK's most beloved seaside destinations — a vibrant city where historic charm meets a lively, contemporary vibe. Whether you're a first-timer or a returning visitor, getting familiar with some key local facts and tips can make your trip smoother, safer, and even more enjoyable. This chapter covers everything you really need to know before and during your stay in Brighton in 2025 — from getting around to what to pack, cultural quirks, and practical advice you won't want to miss.

Getting There and Getting Around

Brighton's excellent connectivity makes it easy to reach and explore:

* **By Train:** The city is just about an hour from London by direct train from London Victoria or London Bridge stations. Brighton Station itself is centrally located, making it a perfect starting point.

* **By Car:** If you're driving, be aware that parking in the city center is limited and expensive. Consider staying at

accommodations that offer parking or use park-and-ride options.

* **Public Transport:** Once in town, buses and e-scooters provide efficient ways to get around. Brighton & Hove Buses cover most neighborhoods, and the compact city center is best explored on foot or by bike — you'll discover many charming streets not accessible by car.

* **Cycling:** Brighton is bike-friendly with dedicated lanes and rental services like "Beryl Bikes" making it easy to zip between attractions.

Where to Stay

Choosing the right neighborhood to stay in can shape your entire experience:

* **The Lanes:** Historic and bustling, perfect for shoppers and food lovers who want to be in the heart of it all.

* **North Laine:** A bohemian hub, great for those seeking independent shops, street art, and vibrant nightlife.

* **Hove:** Quieter and more residential with wide promenades and family-friendly beaches — ideal for a relaxed seaside vibe.

* **Kemp Town:** Chic and colorful, with boutique hotels and a strong café culture.

Weather and What to Pack

Brighton's coastal location means the weather can be unpredictable:

* Summers are generally mild and pleasant but often breezy, so pack layers, including a light windbreaker.

* Winters are relatively mild compared to inland UK, but rain and chill can still surprise you — waterproof footwear and a warm coat are essentials if visiting in the colder months.

* Don't forget comfortable shoes for walking cobblestone streets and the pebbly beach, plus a swimsuit if you're daring enough for a chilly dip in the sea!

Money Matters and Local Currency

* The currency is the British Pound (£). Most places accept contactless payments, including

credit/debit cards and mobile pay options like Apple Pay or Google Pay.

* Some smaller independent shops and market stalls may prefer cash, so it's handy to have some notes on you.

* Brighton has plenty of ATMs, but it's wise to check your bank's international fees before traveling.

Local Culture and Etiquette

Brighton prides itself on being one of the UK's most progressive and welcoming cities, known for its inclusivity, especially its celebrated LGBTQ+ community.

* **Friendly and laid-back:** People in Brighton tend to be open-minded and informal. Don't hesitate to ask locals for recommendations or directions — they're usually happy to help.

* **Sustainability:** Brighton is a leader in sustainable tourism, so do your bit by using reusable water bottles, recycling, and supporting local businesses.

* **Tipping:** While not mandatory, tipping around 10-15% in restaurants and cafés is appreciated if service is good.

Must-Know Local Tips

* **Avoid Peak Times at the Pier:** Brighton Palace Pier is a magnet for tourists. Visit early morning or later in the evening for a more relaxed experience.

* **Markets Are a Must:** Don't miss **Brighton Open Market** and **The Brighton Flea Market** for unique finds and local crafts.

* **Beach Life:** Brighton's famous pebble beach isn't sandy, so bring beach mats or foldable chairs. For a classic seaside day, pack a picnic or try the food stalls along the seafront.

* **Events:** Brighton hosts a packed calendar of events — from the Brighton Festival in May to the lively Brighton Pride in August. Check event dates in advance as accommodation and transport get busier.

Safety and Health

Brighton is generally safe, but as with any busy tourist spot, keep an eye on your belongings, especially in crowded places like the pier or the Lanes.

* Emergency services are reliable; dial 999 for police, fire, or medical emergencies.

* Pharmacies and medical clinics are plentiful; many accept walk-ins.

Connectivity and Staying Online
* Free Wi-Fi is widely available in cafés, libraries, and some public spaces, but having a local SIM or international roaming plan ensures you're always connected.

* Apps like **Citymapper** help navigate public transport routes, while **TimeOut Brighton** or **Visit Brighton** apps keep you updated on events and restaurant openings.

Final Thought: Embrace the Unexpected
Brighton's charm lies in its unpredictability — you might stumble upon a street performer in the Lanes, discover an impromptu art installation, or make a friend over a cup of locally roasted coffee. Being prepared with these essentials gives you the freedom to dive into the city's rhythm without worries.

Take a deep breath of salty air, and remember: Brighton isn't just a destination; it's an experience that grows richer every time you visit.

Staying Connected

In today's world, staying connected during your travels isn't just a convenience — it's essential. Whether you want to keep family updated, navigate Brighton's lively streets with ease, or share your seaside snapshots in real time, having reliable access to communication and digital resources can transform your trip from good to seamless.

Brighton, with its mix of historic charm and modern innovation, offers plenty of options to stay plugged in without hassle. This chapter will guide you through the best ways to keep connected in Brighton in 2025 — from internet access and mobile coverage to digital tools that enrich your experience.

Internet and Wi-fi

Brighton understands that visitors value being online, so free Wi-Fi is quite common, especially in key public areas:

* **Cafés and Coffee Shops:** Many of Brighton's independent cafés and popular chains offer free Wi-Fi to customers. Places like **The Flour Pot Bakery** and **Pelicano**

Coffee not only serve up excellent drinks and pastries but also reliable internet access — perfect for working remotely or uploading your photos.

* **Libraries and Community Spaces:** The **Brighton Jubilee Library** is a great quiet spot with free Wi-Fi and comfortable seating. You can drop in for a few hours to catch up on emails or plan your next day.

* **Public Hotspots:** The city council has expanded free Wi-Fi zones in busy areas such as the **Brighton Palace Pier** and **North Laine**. While it's handy for quick checks, public Wi-Fi can be slower and less secure — so avoid sensitive transactions here.

* **Hotels and Accommodations:** Most hotels, guesthouses, and B\&Bs provide free Wi-Fi. Some upscale hotels also offer dedicated high-speed connections for business travelers or digital nomads.

Tip: Always carry a VPN app on your phone or laptop when using public Wi-Fi to protect your data.

Mobile Coverage and SIM Cards

If you plan to use your mobile phone frequently, whether for calls, navigation, or streaming, consider your options before arriving or soon after:

* **UK Network Providers:** The major UK networks — EE, Vodafone, O2, and Three — all cover Brighton extensively with strong 4G and increasingly available 5G signals. This ensures good connectivity whether you're wandering the city center, walking the beach, or exploring the outskirts.

* **Buying a Local SIM:** For visitors staying a week or longer, picking up a local prepaid SIM card can be a cost-effective way to stay connected. Shops like *Carphone Warehouse* or convenience stores around Brighton Station sell easy-to-activate SIM cards with flexible data packages.

* **International Roaming:** Many providers offer international roaming bundles, but these can be pricey. If you prefer to use your home SIM, check with your carrier for the best deals or consider a dual-SIM phone to use a local SIM alongside your original number.

* **eSIM Options:** For tech-savvy travelers, eSIMs are becoming more popular. Brighton-friendly eSIM providers allow you to purchase data plans online and activate them immediately — no physical card needed.

Useful Apps for Navigating Brighton

Brighton's compact yet vibrant nature means you'll want smart tools to make the most of your time here:

* **Citymapper:** This is the go-to app for public transportation in Brighton. It provides real-time bus routes, schedules, and walking directions, helping you get around quickly without confusion.

* **Beryl Bikes App:** Brighton has embraced bike-sharing with Beryl Bikes scattered across the city. Their app allows you to locate, rent, and pay for bikes instantly — a fantastic way to explore seaside promenades and hidden lanes.

* **Visit Brighton:** The official tourism app offers updates on events, new restaurant openings, and local attractions, plus helpful tips curated by locals.

* **Google Maps:** Still a staple, Google Maps now offers detailed street views of Brighton's unique neighborhoods, from the cobbled Lanes to the colorful Regency architecture of Kemp Town.

* **Weather Apps:** Brighton's coastal weather can shift quickly. Apps like **BBC Weather** or **Met Office** help you plan your day, especially if you're visiting outdoor spots like Brighton Beach or the South Downs.

Sharing Your Brighton Experience

For many travelers, documenting and sharing moments is part of the joy of travel:

* **Photo Spots:** Brighton's photogenic corners are everywhere — from the iconic West Pier ruins at sunset, the quirky street art in North Laine, to the vibrant beach huts at Hove. The best times for photos are early morning or late afternoon when the light softens.

* **Social Media:** Many cafés and shops encourage Instagram-friendly moments with colorful interiors and delicious food displays. Look out for the hashtag #Brighton2025 to connect with locals and other travelers sharing their stories.

* **Local Etiquette:** While Brighton is an open and friendly city, it's always polite to ask before photographing individuals or private properties. Respecting privacy keeps the community welcoming to visitors.

Staying Safe and Secure Online
* Brighton is generally safe, but always be mindful of your digital security.

* Avoid using unsecured public Wi-Fi for banking or confidential transactions.

* Keep your devices charged and bring a portable power bank — especially if you're out exploring the city all day.

Final Thoughts: Balance Connectivity with Presence
While Brighton offers excellent options to stay connected, part of its charm is found in unplugging and soaking up the atmosphere — the salty sea air, the buzz of the quirky shops, the sound of waves hitting the pebbles.

Use your devices as tools to enhance your experience, not distract from it. The best memories often come from spontaneous moments — a chat with a local artist, a street musician's tune, or a quiet stroll on the beach at dusk.

Brighton in 2025 is wired for the modern traveler but still encourages you to pause and savor its unique coastal magic. With these essentials in hand, you'll be well-equipped to stay connected, informed, and safe — all while enjoying every vibrant moment of your seaside escape.

Travel Kindly & Leave No Trace

Brighton is a city that pulses with life—from its colorful streets and vibrant communities to the delicate ecosystems along its pebbled shores and rolling South Downs. As travelers in 2025, the way we visit matters more than ever. This chapter invites you to explore Brighton not only as a destination to be enjoyed but as a living place deserving of your respect and mindful care.

Travel kindly and leave no trace: these principles are simple yet profound, urging us to tread lightly on Brighton's urban and natural landscapes, honor its rich culture, and contribute positively to the communities that call this seaside city home.

The Heart of Responsible Travel in Brighton

Brighton's identity is a beautiful mosaic of history, diversity, and environmental awareness. Once a Victorian spa town, it has transformed into a progressive hub for arts, sustainability, and inclusive culture. This city's ongoing commitment to green initiatives—from zero-waste shops to sustainable transport—means travelers have a unique opportunity to support a future-focused community.

When you walk Brighton's streets, you're stepping into a living story that connects past and present. By traveling kindly, you become part of that narrative—a respectful visitor who honors Brighton's spirit rather than simply passing through.

Respecting the Coastal Environment

Brighton's coastline is iconic but fragile. The famous pebble beach, the remnants of the West Pier, and the adjacent marine life are treasures worth protecting.

* **Avoid Disturbing Wildlife:** Seagulls, shore crabs, and an array of coastal birds call Brighton's beaches home. Observe from a distance and avoid feeding wildlife, as human food disrupts their natural behaviors.

* **Take Your Trash with You:** While the city provides plenty of bins, it's best practice to minimize waste and carry a small reusable bag for any litter until you find a bin. Single-use

plastics are a big issue on the coast; consider alternatives like refillable water bottles and reusable containers.

* **Stay on Designated Paths:** When exploring nearby natural areas such as the South Downs National Park or Stanmer Park, stick to marked trails. These paths protect delicate flora and prevent erosion, preserving the landscape for generations of visitors and locals alike.

Cultural Courtesy: Connecting with Brighton's People

Brighton thrives on its welcoming and diverse community, but kindness is a two-way street.

* **Support Local Businesses:** The city's independent shops, cafes, and markets are the heartbeat of its economy. Choosing to buy handmade goods or dine at family-run restaurants helps sustain local livelihoods and keeps Brighton's character vibrant.

* **Engage with Respect:** Whether you're chatting with street performers in The Lanes or attending a community event, approach with genuine curiosity and an open heart. Brighton's residents are proud of their inclusive and

creative culture; reciprocate by listening and respecting their stories and spaces.

* **Be Mindful of Noise:** Brighton's nightlife is lively, but when you return to quieter neighborhoods like Hanover or Kemptown, keep noise levels considerate, especially late at night.

Sustainable Transport: Move Lightly Around Town

Brighton is a leader in sustainable urban mobility, making it easy and enjoyable to explore without a car.

* **Cycle or Walk:** The city offers extensive cycling lanes and pedestrian-friendly routes. Renting a bike through the Beryl Bikes app or taking leisurely strolls allows you to soak up the city's charm while reducing your carbon footprint.

* **Public Transport:** Brighton's buses are efficient and run frequently between key spots like the station, seafront, and university areas. Using public transport reduces traffic congestion and pollution.

* **Electric Options:** Increasingly, electric taxis and car clubs are available for those who need motorized transport. Opting for electric vehicles helps Brighton move towards its goal of net-zero emissions by 2030.

Leave a Positive Impact

Travel kindness goes beyond just minimizing harm—it's about actively giving back.

* **Volunteer Locally:** Brighton hosts numerous community projects, from beach clean-ups to arts initiatives. If you have time, look for short-term volunteering opportunities—you'll meet locals and make a tangible difference.

* **Choose Ethical Accommodations:** Many hotels and guesthouses in Brighton now focus on sustainability—using renewable energy, reducing waste, and supporting local suppliers. Staying in eco-conscious lodging supports these efforts.

* **Practice Mindful Consumption:** When shopping or dining, consider the origins of your purchases. Brighton's emphasis on organic, fair-trade, and vegan-friendly products reflects a wider ethical stance that visitors can join in.

Visitors who travel kindly often share how their respectful choices enhanced their experience. For example, one traveler recounts a spontaneous moment on Brighton Pier when, after picking up litter, a local thanked them warmly and shared insider tips on hidden art galleries nearby. Another recalls attending a community storytelling night in a tucked-away café, feeling welcomed not just as a tourist, but as a participant in Brighton's vibrant cultural dialogue.

These stories remind us that mindful travel enriches both visitor and host, creating memories grounded in connection and care.

Final Thoughts: Your Role in Brighton's Future

Brighton is more than a postcard-perfect seaside town. It's a dynamic, living city balancing growth and conservation, tradition and innovation. Your journey here matters—how you explore, engage, and impact this special place shapes its future.

Travel kindly: honor Brighton's environment, embrace its cultural richness, and leave only footprints of respect behind. By doing so, you help ensure this beloved city remains a shining example of coastal charm and conscious living for decades to come.

Day Trips and Nearby Destinations

Brighton's magnetic charm might just tempt you to linger within its vibrant streets and lively seafront—but the real magic begins when you venture beyond. In 2025, this coastal city serves as a perfect launchpad to explore the rich tapestry of nearby landscapes, historic towns, and nature escapes that pepper Sussex and the South Downs.

Whether you crave ancient castles, windswept beaches, or quaint villages bursting with English charm, the surrounding region offers day trips that ignite your curiosity and satisfy your thirst for discovery. This chapter is your passport to uncovering the best of Brighton's neighborhood adventures—packed with stories, secrets, and sights you'll want to share long after you return.

1. Arundel: A Journey Back in Time

Just under an hour's drive west of Brighton lies Arundel, a picture-perfect market town that seems pulled straight from a storybook.

Dominated by the imposing silhouette of Arundel Castle, this destination invites you to step into centuries of English history.

* **Arundel Castle:** Spend a few hours exploring the lovingly preserved castle grounds, with their sweeping views of the South Downs and the River Arun. The castle's interiors are filled with antiques, tapestries, and a fascinating collection of paintings. History buffs will especially enjoy the guided tours, which weave in tales of medieval intrigue and aristocratic grandeur.

* **Stroll through the Town:** Wander the narrow streets lined with independent shops, artisan galleries, and cozy tearooms. The town's annual events, like the Arundel Festival in summer, infuse the streets with lively music and local crafts—ideal for timing your visit.

* **Insider Tip:** Head to a café overlooking the river for a late afternoon cup of tea. Watch as the light shifts over the water—an evocative moment that encapsulates why day trips like this feel so timeless.

2. The Seven Sisters and Beachy Head: Nature's Dramatic Playground If breathtaking coastal landscapes stir your soul, a trip east to the Seven Sisters cliffs and Beachy Head is non-negotiable.

* **Seven Sisters Country Park:** Just a 40-minute drive from Brighton, the chalk-white cliffs offer some of the most stunning seaside walks in England. The contrast of vivid green meadows above against the sparkling English Channel below is spectacular any time of year.

* **Hiking and Photography:** Pack your walking shoes and camera. Trails here range from gentle strolls to more adventurous hikes, all offering panoramic views that photographers dream about.

* **Beachy Head Lighthouse:** Don't miss the lighthouse perched at the foot of the cliffs, accessible via a steep path. This iconic structure has been guiding ships since the 19th century and now stands as a symbol of the area's wild beauty.

* **Safety Note:** The cliffs are dramatic but fragile; stay well behind barriers and avoid loose edges, especially on windy days.

3. Lewes: Quirky, Historic, and Full of Surprises

Less than 30 minutes by train or car from Brighton, Lewes is a charming town steeped in history and bursting with character.

* **Lewes Castle and Museums:** Climb the motte for sweeping views, then explore the castle's museum that narrates local stories, including the town's rebellious spirit during the Peasants' Revolt.

* **Independent Spirit:** Lewes is famed for its eclectic shops, bookstores, and cafes. Spend an afternoon browsing vinyl records or handmade ceramics, then unwind with a craft beer at one of the town's many microbreweries.

* **Bonfire Night Tradition:** If your trip coincides with November, experiencing Lewes Bonfire Night is unforgettable—the town's raucous and colorful celebrations are a vivid expression of local pride and tradition.

4. Devil's Dyke: A Hilltop Escape with Endless Views

For a quick nature fix, head to Devil's Dyke, a short 20-minute drive north of Brighton.

* **Why Visit:**yThis ancient dry valley in the South Downs offers some of the most breathtaking panoramic views in Sussex. On a clear day, you can see the English Channel, the Isle of Wight, and even London's skyline far in the distance.

* **Activities:** Devil's Dyke is a haven for walkers, paragliders, and picnickers. The café at the visitor center serves local snacks and hot drinks—perfect for refueling after a brisk walk.

* **Storytelling Moment:** Legend has it that the valley was created by the Devil himself, whose wrath supposedly gouged the land in an act of fury. Whether you believe it or not, the landscape's drama invites your imagination to roam free.

5. Hastings: Seaside History Meets Creative Revival

A little further afield, about an hour by train, Hastings offers a blend of historic intrigue and modern cultural buzz.

* **Old Town:** Explore the winding alleys where medieval architecture lives alongside vibrant street art. Quaint pubs and seafood shacks invite you to savor the local catch while absorbing the town's salty air.

* **Battle of Hastings Connection:** History fans can visit the nearby site of the famous 1066 battle, with exhibitions and reenactments bringing this pivotal moment in English history to life.

* **Creative Scene:** Hastings has undergone a creative renaissance, with new galleries, live music venues, and craft markets that make it a rewarding destination for art lovers.

Practical Tips for Your Day Trips

* **Getting There:** Many of these destinations are easily accessible by train, bus, or car from Brighton. The South Downs Way, a long-distance footpath, also connects several key points for walkers.

* **Pack Smart:** Weather can change quickly on the coast and in the hills. Layered clothing, sturdy shoes, and a refillable water bottle are essentials.

* **Timing:** Start early to make the most of your day, especially in summer when popular spots can get busy. Off-peak visits offer a quieter, more intimate experience.

Final Thoughts: Your Adventure, Your Story

Brighton may be your base, but the surrounding landscapes and towns offer endless possibilities to expand your journey. Each day trip is a chance to uncover a new facet of English heritage, nature, and culture—all within a short distance. Let curiosity guide you, embrace the unexpected, and collect stories that will make your trip to Brighton truly unforgettable.

Photo-Worthy Moments

Brighton isn't just a city you visit; it's a living canvas waiting for your creative eye. In 2025, this vibrant seaside town blends history, whimsy, and modern energy into a tapestry that invites photographers, artists, and daydreamers alike to capture its essence. From the sun-kissed pebbles of the beach to the kaleidoscope of colors in its street art, Brighton offers an endless gallery of photo-worthy moments that tell stories beyond what words can convey.

Whether you wield a professional camera, a trusty smartphone, or simply a curious eye, Brighton's diverse scenes invite you to pause, look closer, and frame your own interpretation of this seaside escape.

The Iconic Brighton Palace Pier — Nostalgia and Motion

Start your photographic journey with the unmistakable silhouette of the Brighton Palace Pier. This historic pier, built in 1899, is a place where nostalgia and life dance side by side.

* **Golden Hour Magic:**Arrive just before sunset when the fading light softens the colors and casts long shadows over the sea. The arcade lights start to twinkle, and the laughter of families blends with the salty breeze—a perfect moment to capture warmth and joy.

* **Candid Street Scenes:** Don't just focus on the structures. Snap candid portraits of street performers, couples strolling hand in hand, or children delighting in the carousel. These human moments add soul to your collection.

* **Tip:** Experiment with long exposures to blur the motion of the waves against the pier's legs, creating an ethereal effect that contrasts beautifully with the solid architecture.

The Vibrant Lanes

Venture into Brighton's Lanes, a labyrinth of narrow alleys packed with independent shops, cafés, and vibrant street art that pulse with creativity.

* **Textures and Details:** The Lanes are a feast for macro and detail shots—think close-ups of vintage shop signs, weathered brick walls layered with murals, or intricately patterned doorways.

* **Morning Light:** Early morning offers soft, diffused lighting and fewer crowds, allowing you to capture the charming emptiness of these historic streets. Coffee steam rising from a café cup on a windowsill can add a poetic touch.

* **Unexpected Discoveries:** Keep your eyes peeled for quirky window displays or a splash of unexpected color—a pastel-painted door, an antique bicycle leaning against a wall, or a street artist's palette.

Under the West Pier

Just a short walk from the Palace Pier, the West Pier stands in haunting ruin, a skeletal monument to Brighton's past. In 2025, it remains one of the city's most evocative subjects.

* **Dramatic Skies:** The best time to visit is during overcast or stormy weather when the dark clouds add drama and moodiness to your compositions. The pier's iron framework juxtaposed against turbulent skies speaks of resilience and time's passage.

* **Silhouettes and Shadows:** As the sun dips, the pier's remains cast long shadows across the beach, perfect for high-contrast black-and-white photography that captures the pier's ghostly allure.

* **Pro Tip:** Try shooting from the beach at low tide to include the wet sand reflections, adding a surreal depth to your shots.

Brighton Beach and the Pebbles

Brighton's beach is a mosaic of smooth, rounded pebbles, creating a unique texture that's both tactile and visually captivating.

* **Abstract Art:** Focus your lens on the patterns formed by pebbles—wet stones glistening in the sunlight, or the intricate swirls of foam as waves kiss the shore. These abstract images tell the story of Brighton's natural charm.

* **Classic Seaside Portraits:** Capture families and friends enjoying the quintessential seaside experience—kite flying, ice cream licking, or simply lounging on striped deck chairs. The colorful beach huts in the background add joyful pops of color.

* **Seasonal Shifts:** Each season offers a different beach vibe—golden summers buzzing with life, quiet autumn mornings with misty horizons, or crisp winter days with frosted pebbles.

Royal Pavilion Gardens

No photo collection of Brighton is complete without the stunning Royal Pavilion and its gardens. This exotic palace, built for the Prince Regent in the early 19th century, is a flamboyant fusion of Indian and Chinese architectural styles.

* **Architectural Wonder:** The Pavilion's onion domes and ornate facades make for striking architectural photography. Play with angles and framing to highlight its unique features against the sky.

* **Garden Serenity:** Surrounding the Pavilion, the gardens offer lush greenery, tranquil ponds, and exotic plants that change throughout the year. Capture reflections, dew drops, or sun-dappled pathways for a softer, peaceful contrast to the palace's extravagance.

* **Cultural Layers:** Look for visitors in traditional dress during cultural festivals or local events—these moments enrich your photos with stories of Brighton's diverse community.

Street Art and the Creative Spirit

Brighton's commitment to supporting local artists has transformed many parts of the city into ever-evolving open-air galleries.

* **North Laine:** This bohemian neighborhood is your go-to spot for colorful murals, provocative graffiti, and thought-provoking installations. Each piece reflects the city's spirit of inclusivity and rebellion.

* **Changing Scenes:** Street art is ephemeral. What you photograph today might be replaced tomorrow, making your shots precious documents of Brighton's living art scene.

* **Interactive Shots:** Engage with local artists if you can—many are happy to share their inspiration and even pose for portraits alongside their work.

Brighton invites you to slow down and see the ordinary transformed into the extraordinary. It's a city that rewards patience, curiosity, and a willingness to see beauty in contrasts—the old and new, the natural and man-made, the calm and the vibrant. As you wander through its streets, beaches, and hidden corners, remember that every photo you take is more than just an image—it's your personal story, your artistic footprint on this ever-changing seaside canvas.

So charge your camera, wear comfortable shoes, and let Brighton inspire you to create moments that linger long after the shutter clicks.

Packing Smart for Brighton

Getting Ready for Your Brighton Adventure

So, your Brighton getaway is officially on the horizon—fantastic choice! Whether you're heading here for the pebbled beaches, indie art scene, or charming historic lanes, one thing's for sure: packing smart will make your trip smoother, lighter, and way more enjoyable.

In 2025, Brighton continues to blend quirky seaside fun with sophisticated culture, offering everything from music festivals and Pride parades to lazy days at beach cafés and peaceful strolls along the South Downs. But thanks to its unpredictable coastal weather and an eclectic mix of activities, Brighton is the kind of place where it pays to pack with purpose.

Weather-Wise Wardrobe

If there's one truth every Brighton local agrees on, it's that the weather can't be trusted. Sunshine in the morning might turn into seaside gusts by afternoon. To stay comfortable and ready for anything, layers are key.

* **Light Jacket or Windbreaker:** Essential, even in summer. The sea breeze can be surprisingly chilly, especially along the promenade or on boat rides to the Marina.

* **Waterproof Gear:** Brighton's coastal location means rain can roll in without much warning. A compact, breathable raincoat or a small travel umbrella will be your best allies. Bonus points if it's stylish—this is Brighton, after all!

* **Comfy Footwear:** Whether you're navigating cobbled streets in The Lanes or taking the scenic Undercliff Walk to Saltdean, good walking shoes are a must. Waterproof trainers or low-profile hiking shoes work well for most excursions.

* **Mix-and-Match Basics:** Pack clothes you can layer and reuse—think jeans, t-shirts, and a couple of breathable long-sleeves. Brighton's fashion is relaxed, expressive, and a little bohemian, so don't be afraid to throw in a funky scarf or patterned shirt to match the local vibe.

Tech and Gadgets

Brighton in 2025 is tech-savvy but still delightfully unplugged in places. If you're planning to navigate the city, capture its beauty, and keep in touch, a few key items will serve you well.

* **Universal Travel Adapter (for international visitors):** The UK uses Type G plugs, and Brighton accommodations are modern, but it's still a good idea to bring your own.
* **Portable Power Bank:** Between snapping photos of the Royal Pavilion, streaming the Brighton Festival lineup, and navigating with Google Maps, your phone will get a workout. A reliable power bank keeps you going all day.
* **Camera or Smartphone with Extra Storage:** Brighton's streets, sunsets, and surprise moments (like the saxophonist under the pier or a spontaneous beach drum circle) beg to be captured. Bring a phone with plenty of space or a lightweight camera with a zoom lens.

Beach and Day Trip Essentials

Even if you're not the sunbathing type, you'll likely spend plenty of time near Brighton's iconic shoreline. While it's a pebble beach (so no need for sand-resistant gadgets), packing for a Brighton beach day is still a smart move.

* **Beach Blanket or Mat:** Something compact and cushioned will make sitting on the pebbles much more comfortable.
* **Swimsuit & Towel:** Brave enough for a dip in the English Channel? Go for it! Many visitors take advantage of Brighton's beach saunas or try paddleboarding and kayaking.
* **Sunscreen & Sunglasses:** Even on cloudy days, UV rays reflect off the water. A high-SPF sunscreen and good sunglasses are year-round necessities.
* **Reusable Water Bottle:** Hydration is key, especially if you're cycling the seafront or walking through the hilly Seven Dials neighborhood. Brighton is very eco-conscious, and refill stations are available around town.

Culture and Nightlife Must-Haves

Brighton's social calendar is always buzzing—art exhibitions in the North Laine, indie gigs at Concorde 2, pub nights in Kemptown, or elegant dinners near Hove Lawns. You'll want to be prepared for a wide range of experiences.

* **Smart-Casual Outfit:** Most places are relaxed, but a nice outfit will come in handy for cocktails on a rooftop terrace or a night out at Brighton Dome.

* **Compact Tote or Crossbody Bag:** Perfect for shopping the Lanes or carrying your essentials on a night out. Pickpocketing is rare, but secure zips give peace of mind in busy festival crowds.

* **Notebook or Journal:** With Brighton's rich character and the creative energy in the air, you might find yourself inspired to sketch, write, or jot down a favorite café's name. Analog is still charming here.

Sustainable Travel Tools

Brighton prides itself on being one of the greenest cities in the UK, and travelers are encouraged to tread lightly and travel kindly.

* **Reusable Shopping Bag:** From the Saturday farmers' market at Brighton Open Market to vintage treasure hunts at Snoopers Paradise, you'll appreciate a foldable bag.

* **Bamboo Cutlery/Reusable Coffee Cup:** Brighton's many food stalls and indie coffee houses often give discounts to customers who bring their own cups or utensils.

* **Eco-Friendly Toiletries:** Many accommodations offer plastic-free toiletries, but packing your own shampoo bar, solid deodorant, or biodegradable soap adds to your sustainable travel ethos.

A Few Brighton-Specific Extras
Finally, a few items that are surprisingly helpful (and a bit quirky) in Brighton:

* **Small Change or Contactless Card:** Most places are contactless-friendly, but keep a couple of pound coins handy—especially for old-school arcade games on the pier or buskers.

* **Travel App Downloads:** Download the Brighton & Hove Buses app and the Brighton Museum & Art Gallery guide to enhance your local experiences with ease.

* **An Open Mind:** Okay, you can't pack this—but keep it with you. Brighton thrives on diversity, self-expression, and community. Whether you're dancing at Pride, chatting with locals at a poetry night, or trying vegan fish and chips for the first time, lean into the experience.

With your thoughtfully packed bag and a heart full of excitement, you're all set for the many adventures Brighton has to offer. Packing smart means you can travel light, move freely, and fully immerse yourself in every delightful, quirky, and charming moment this seaside gem brings your way.

And remember: if you forget anything, Brighton's eclectic shops and friendly locals have got you covered.

Emergency & Essential Contacts

Peace of Mind on the South Coast

Brighton is known for its charm, colour, and creativity—but even in a vibrant and welcoming place like this, it's comforting to know that help is always within reach. Whether it's a lost wallet, a sudden illness, or a late-night train query, having the right contacts and knowing where to turn can make all the difference.

This chapter isn't just a list of phone numbers—it's your pocket safety net, woven with local insights to help you navigate unexpected hiccups calmly and confidently. Think of it as your gentle travel guardian: quiet, dependable, and ready when you need it.

In Case of Emergency
Who to Call and Where to Go

Let's start with the basics. In the UK, the emergency number is **999**—this connects you to **police**, **ambulance**, **fire services**, and **coastguard**. It's free to call from any phone, mobile or landline, and operates 24/7.

* **Medical Emergencies**: Call 999 if you or someone nearby is in serious danger—this includes chest pain, difficulty breathing, or unconsciousness.

* **Non-Emergency Medical Help:** Dial **111** for NHS 111, a free service offering urgent but non-life-threatening medical advice. They can direct you to a GP, pharmacist, or local clinic.

Nearest Major Hospital:
* **Royal Sussex County Hospital**
   Eastern Road, Brighton, BN2 5BE
   +44 (0)1273 696955
This is Brighton's largest hospital, complete with an Accident & Emergency department, located near Kemptown and easily accessible by bus or taxi.

Safety in the City
Police and Personal Security
Brighton is considered a safe city for visitors, thanks to its friendly local culture and well-lit public spaces. Still, like in any bustling destination, petty theft can occasionally occur—especially in crowded areas like The Lanes, Churchill Square, or Brighton Station.

* **Sussex Police Non-Emergency Line:** 101

For lost property, reporting non-urgent incidents, or requesting community assistance.
* **Brighton Police Station (John Street)**
  John Street, Brighton, BN2 0LA
  +44 (0)1273 404935

If you've lost your passport, the police can issue a report that may be required by your embassy to reissue travel documents.

Health & Wellbeing
When You're Feeling Under the Weather
Travel often brings surprises—and sometimes, they include sniffles or a twisted ankle after a long walk along the Undercliff Path. Brighton's health services are accessible, kind, and efficient, with options for both residents and visitors.

Walk-In Medical Clinics (for minor injuries and ailments):
* **Brighton Station Health Centre**
  Aspect House, 84-87 Queens Road, BN1 3XE
  +44 (0)300 303 8500
  Open 8am to 8pm daily; just steps from the station, this is the go-to for walk-in GP services.

Pharmacies

Pharmacies are dotted throughout the city, often open late. Boots (Western Road), Superdrug (North Street), and a number of independent chemists carry essentials and provide advice on over-the-counter medications.

Mental Health Support

Brighton's progressive culture includes a strong focus on mental wellness. For immediate emotional support:

* **Samaritans (24/7 helpline): 116 123** (free)
* **Mind in Brighton & Hove:** +44 (0)1273 666950

You'll find Brighton to be a very open and non-judgmental space to reach out for help if you need it.

Lost or Stolen Items

It's surprisingly easy to leave your phone on a bench at Brighton Pier or misplace your wallet during a lively night at a beachfront bar. If it happens, don't panic—Brighton has systems in place to help.

* Lost Property – Brighton Station:
+44 (0)3457 484950 (Southern Rail)

Visit in person at the station's customer service desk or report online.

* Lost Property – Brighton & Hove Buses:
+44 (0)1273 886200

Items found on city buses are stored at the Conway Street depot in Hove. Allow a day or two for items to be logged.

Tip: Make digital backups of your ID and keep emergency cash in a separate bag.

Travel Help: Trains, Taxis, and Getting Around Safely

Brighton Railway Station is a hub of comings and goings. Staff here are friendly and used to helping travelers navigate ticket machines, platform changes, and missed connections.

* National Rail Inquiries: 03457 48 49 50
* Southern Rail Customer Services: 03451 27 29 20

Brighton & Hove Buses are reliable and cover every corner of the city. Drivers are approachable, and the mobile app shows live times and route planning.

* **Brighton & Hove Bus App :** Free on iOS and Android
* **Customer Service :** +44 (0)1273 886200

Taxis and Ride Services:
* **Brighton Streamline Taxis :** +44 (0)1273 20 20 20
    You can book in advance or hail a cab at stands near the station or Old Steine.
* **Uber:** operates in Brighton as well, although local taxi firms often offer faster service in peak times.

Embassy Support and International Assistance
If you're visiting from abroad and lose your passport, fall ill, or need consular support, your nearest embassy may be in **London.** That's just an hour by train from Brighton.

* **Check the UK Government Foreign Embassies Directory:**
[www.gov.uk/world/embassies]
(https://www.gov.uk/world/embassies)

* Or use **your home country's consulate website** for contact information and services for citizens abroad.

Many embassies offer 24/7 emergency hotlines for their nationals.

Local Lifesavers

Sometimes, help doesn't wear a uniform. Brighton's community spirit shines through in small acts—like a barista at a North Laine café who'll lend you their charger, or the beach cleaner who offers directions when you're lost.

Look for

* **Brighton Ambassadors:** During festivals and summer weekends, these friendly volunteers roam high-traffic areas to assist tourists with directions and local tips.

* **Libraries and Community Centres:** Places like **Jubilee Library** in central Brighton often have free Wi-Fi, public restrooms, and helpful staff for general guidance.

While we hope your trip is smooth sailing, knowing where to turn when things go awry brings peace of mind. In Brighton, you're never far from help—and often, that help comes with a warm smile and a reassuring accent.

So keep this chapter bookmarked, pack your curiosity alongside your confidence, and step into Brighton's energy with a calm heart. You've got this—and Brighton's got you.

Useful Apps and Websites

Your Digital Toolkit for a Smarter Brighton Experience

Brighton might wear the charm of a quirky Victorian seaside town, but don't be fooled—this coastal gem is thoroughly plugged into the modern world. In 2025, traveling smart doesn't just mean packing the right shoes for beach strolls or bringing a reusable water bottle. It means having the best digital tools at your fingertips to navigate, explore, and immerse yourself in Brighton like a local—with less hassle and more fun.

From apps that guide you through The Lanes' twisty alleys to websites that uncover secret supper clubs in Hanover, Brighton's tech scene meets its vibrant culture head-on. This chapter rounds up the most helpful and up-to-date digital companions to enhance your stay—each one tested, loved, and ready for your download list.

Getting Around
Brighton & Hove Buses App
If you're relying on public transport (and you should—it's efficient and eco-friendly), this app is a must. It offers live bus times, route maps, ticket purchases, and even alerts when you're nearing your stop. Bonus: You can plan multi-stop journeys across town and save your favourite routes, perfect for hopping from North Laine's vintage shops to the seafront.

Pro Tip: The "M-ticket" function lets you buy tickets in advance and just scan your phone when boarding.

Trainline
For day trips to London, Lewes, or the South Downs, Trainline remains the go-to rail app. It shows real-time departures, platform numbers, and fare comparisons. Trains to and from Brighton Station can get crowded during festivals and weekends, so use the app's crowd predictor and book seats ahead.

Exploring the City: Find the Cool Stuff Faster, VisitBrighton.com
The city's official tourism website has evolved beautifully in 2025. Its sleek interface now includes interactive maps, neighborhood

breakdowns, and curated itineraries for every type of traveler—families, foodies, solo wanderers, and LGBTQ+ adventurers. Their "What's On" calendar is particularly handy for discovering pop-up events, outdoor cinema nights, and hidden gallery openings.

Insider Feature: The "Local Stories" section features mini-interviews with Brighton creatives, giving you a deeper connection to the culture.

Komoot

This is a hiker and biker's dream app, and Brighton is full of routes begging to be explored—from the Undercliff Walk stretching toward Saltdean to forest trails near Stanmer Park. Komoot's turn-by-turn directions, difficulty ratings, and downloadable offline maps make it ideal for escaping the city bustle without getting lost.

Food & Drink: Skip the Chains, Find the Gems

Brighton's sustainability ethos pairs perfectly with this app, which lets you rescue end-of-day meals from cafés, bakeries, and restaurants at discounted prices. From a surprise vegan feast from Food for Friends to leftover pastries at

Flour Pot Bakery, this app satisfies your hunger while saving food waste.

Brighton Food Tours (Website & Booking Tool)
Their website is a launchpad into Brighton's indie food scene. Not only can you book guided tasting walks, but you'll also find blog posts and downloadable food maps tailored to niche cravings—like a gluten-free sweet trail or craft beer crawl through Kemptown.

Local Highlight: Use their seasonal produce guide if you're visiting Brighton's Open Market and want to sample what's fresh and local.

Nightlife & Culture: From Quiet Jazz to Queer Cabaret

Ents24
While many travelers still rely on ticketing giants, Brighton locals swear by Ents24 for finding off-the-radar gigs, underground theatre, and comedy nights. It pulls listings from dozens of venues and allows alerts for your favorite performers. Venues like The Hope & Ruin, Komedia, and Patterns regularly post here before anywhere else.

DesignMyNight

This site and app combo is your personal nightlife concierge. Whether you're in the mood for a speakeasy with live piano or an immersive drag bingo event, it has filters by vibe, price range, and even dress code. Book tables, buy tickets, and save your spots with a few taps.

Staying Connected: Local Services & Safety

Brighton Wi-Fi Map (via City Council Website)

Free public Wi-Fi is widely available in Brighton—especially in hotspots like the seafront, Pavilion Gardens, and Churchill Square. The city council's updated 2025 digital map marks every available hotspot, plus signal strength and hours of availability. It's a lifesaver if you're trying to conserve data or work remotely from a sunny bench.

Citymapper (Brighton Mode)

New in 2025: Brighton has been added to Citymapper's growing list of smart urban navigation apps. It includes walking, bus, cycling, and even electric scooter routing. Great for first-time visitors who want to compare commute times and get ETA estimates that account for real-time traffic or seafront road closures.

Accommodation & Neighborhood Vibes

Airbnb & Booking.com – with a Brighton Filter Twist

While the platforms themselves are familiar, Brighton's local hosts have really leaned into curation. On Airbnb, you'll find listings that come with yoga mats, vinyl players, or rooftop terraces overlooking the marina. Booking.com now features "Sustainability Badges," helping you choose green-certified stays around eco-conscious neighborhoods like Hanover or Fiveways.

Nextdoor (Brighton Group)

Want to feel more like a resident than a tourist? The Brighton section of this community-based social app is full of hyper-local tips—from where to find the best sourdough to alerts about impromptu drum circles at Brighton Beach. It's a real-time pulse of the city from the people who live it every day.

In Case You Need Help use the NHS App
If you're from the UK, you likely already have this app to access medical care. For international visitors, the NHS 111 website is mobile-optimized and user-friendly, offering symptom checkers and pharmacy locators.

What3Words
Brighton has dozens of winding alleys, secret gardens, and quirky corners—pinpointing your exact location can be tricky, especially if you're meeting friends or calling a taxi. This app assigns a unique three-word address to every 3x3m square of the city. Whether you're at "funky.lime.biscuit" in The Lanes or "ocean.flip.lantern" by the Pier, you'll never be lost in translation again.

The Smart Way to Travel Brighton
With the right digital tools in your pocket, Brighton becomes even more accessible, fun, and personalized. These apps and websites don't replace serendipitous discovery—they enhance it. So go ahead and get techy, stay spontaneous, and let Brighton's pixels and personality lead the way.

Farewell Notes

A Seaside Goodbye That Lingers Long After the Waves

As your Brighton journey draws to a close, it's hard not to feel that gentle tug of reluctance—the one that whispers, just one more stroll along the seafront... one more coffee in a sun-dappled café... one more glance at the ever-changing English Channel. Brighton has that effect on people. It doesn't just charm you while you're here; it nestles into your memory, becoming a place you carry with you long after you've returned home.

Whether you've spent a long weekend here or let the city unfold over several weeks, Brighton leaves footprints in the heart. In these farewell notes, we take a moment to reflect on what makes this vibrant coastal enclave so hard to leave, and why—somehow—it always calls us back.

The Soundtrack of the Sea

Brighton is, above all else, a city defined by the rhythm of the sea. Every walk along the promenade has its own melody: the cries of gulls overhead, the gentle percussion of pebbles shifting under waves, the distant thrum of a busker's guitar by the Pier.

On your last evening, take a slow walk from Hove Lawns back toward the Brighton Palace Pier. Watch as the sky shifts from sapphire to rose gold. Locals will tell you: **Brighton's best conversations happen while walking by the sea.** Whether you're alone, lost in your own thoughts, or with someone you love, the seafront has a way of grounding you—reminding you of simple joys and the value of stillness.

Echoes from the Lanes and North Laine
If the seafront is Brighton's heartbeat, then The Lanes and North Laine are its soul. As you pack your suitcase with trinkets from local boutiques—perhaps a handmade ring from a North Laine jeweller or a rare vinyl from Resident Records—you're also taking a piece of Brighton's creative spirit with you.

Don't forget the moments between the souvenirs: that surprise conversation with a shopkeeper who shared their favorite quiet pub in Kemptown, or the impromptu laughter that bubbled up while squeezing through the impossibly narrow Twitten alleyways.

Brighton's indie identity isn't just in its wares—it's in the warmth of the people who make and share them.

Flavours You'll Crave Again

Few people leave Brighton without a new favorite dish—or ten. Maybe it was that breakfast shakshuka at Café Coho that gave you the perfect start to your day. Or the vegan mezze from Earth & Stars that changed your mind about plant-based dining altogether.

The city's food scene is so varied, it often becomes a kind of culinary passport—offering tastes of India, Lebanon, Ethiopia, and Italy all within walking distance. And somehow, even the humble fish and chips by the Pier taste better in Brighton—wrapped in paper, eaten on a bench, and shared with a friend or two (plus a hopeful seagull hovering nearby).

Brighton's People: Eccentric, Kind, and Unapologetically Themselves

One of the most striking things about Brighton is how effortlessly it embraces difference. Whether you're wandering through a drag show at Charles Street Tap or catching a poetry slam at Komedia, you'll feel that unmistakable freedom in the air—an unspoken invitation to be exactly who you are.

Perhaps you made a connection with a gallery owner in the Artists Quarter or struck up a conversation with a friendly local while waiting in line for gelato. Brighton's people are often a little quirky, always interesting, and refreshingly open. That feeling—that you belong here, even as a visitor—is one of the city's greatest gifts.

Seasons and Stories: A City That Shifts and Shines

As you look back on your time here, think about how Brighton met you. Maybe it was in spring, with the cherry blossoms in Preston Park bursting into bloom. Or perhaps it was summer, when the beaches buzzed with life, laughter, and music festivals echoing from every corner of the city.

Each season tells its own Brighton story. Autumn brings golden leaves to Pavilion Gardens and quieter cafés where locals sip mulled cider. Winter wraps the city in cozy light, with ice-skating beneath the Royal Pavilion's spires and festive markets down by the Marina. No matter when you visited,

Brighton left you with a unique chapter of its ever-evolving narrative.

If there's time, take a final dip in the sea—yes, even if it's chilly. Join the locals at Sea Lanes or the swimmers at Saltdean Lido and feel the cold wash over you. It's not just invigorating; it's a baptism into the Brighton way of life: bold, present, and deeply connected to nature.

Before boarding your train at Brighton Station, glance up at the clock tower and listen to the hum of people heading in all directions. Your visit is ending, but Brighton doesn't stand still. It will continue—colorful, musical, delicious, eccentric, loving—waiting to welcome you again.

Parting Words

Brighton isn't just a destination; it's a feeling. A city where pebble beaches meet street art, where 19th-century architecture hugs cutting-edge culture, and where the skies over the sea stretch wider than you remembered they could. It teaches you to slow down, to savor the offbeat, and to seek out the human connections in every encounter.

So, as you leave, don't say goodbye. Say "see you later." Because Brighton doesn't end when you zip your suitcase—it lingers in the scent of sea air on your clothes, the song stuck in your head from a gig at The Green Door Store, and the fresh perspective you take back home.

Whenever you're ready, Brighton will still be here. Evolving, surprising, embracing.

Until next time—farewell, and thank you for making memories by the sea.

– Abigail I Andrea

Printed in Dunstable, United Kingdom

68478760R00107